What people are saying about this book

"I have carefully read and reviewed the collective research compiled and featured in this book. I found it to be factual and quite impressive. I totally support Chad Lewis and Terry Fisk in their book titled The Wisconsin Road Guide To Haunted Locations. *I wish them continued success in their efforts to promote credible ghost research."*

Peter James - Psychic, host of the television series *Ghost Encounters,* and author of *Heaven Can You Hear Me?*

****

"Being a medium, one of the things that I enjoy is a good haunted location. Not only is a good haunt thrilling but it's a story waiting to be uncovered. The Wisconsin Road Guide to Haunted Locations *serves as a detailed guide to allow you to sample not only the unknown but a piece of history. This book was written with its readers in mind providing you with a delicious account of actual hauntings and reminding us all that both living and dead cross paths every day. This book is both thought provoking and a great conversation piece."*

Allison DuBois - Human Energy System's Laboratory Research Medium, subject of NBC's television series *Medium* and author of *Don't Kiss Them Good-Bye*

****

"At last. Wisconsin has an exhaustive sourcebook for paranormal places and events that cuts through legendary shadows, yanks the skeletons from their dank closets and examines each instance in an even-handed way. Terry Fisk and Chad Lewis are no armchair investigators, and their impeccable fieldwork has enabled them to put together an invaluable resource for anyone casting a hairy eyeball toward the unexplained. A must-have for actual or vicarious road trips in search of the Dairy State's stranger side."

Linda Godfrey - Author of *The Beast of Bray Road, Tailing Wisconsin's Werewolf; The Poison Widow, A True Story of Sin, Strychnine and Murder;* and co-author of *Weird Wisconsin, Your Travel Guide to Wisconsin's Best Kept Secrets and Local Legends*

****

"I have known Chad and Terry for many years now and as you pick this fantastic book up and read about the secret scary places of Wisconsin, be reassured that integrity was put into each page. When the hair on the back of your head raises, there will be a part of you that just wants to believe, for it could be real. Who knows—you just might want to join them on their next adventure into the unknown, enjoy."

Michael T. Coffield - Futurist, host of *Back Page News*

****

"Finally, a directory of Wisconsin haunts! Lewis and Fisk have compiled scores of local haunts and legend along with descriptive investigative notes and locations. Their style allows the reader to decide whether the story is fact or mere fiction. Definitely, a must have for any ghost researcher or enthusiast. Simply, an intriguing publication."

Shawn Blaschka - Investigator, Wausau Paranormal Research Society

THE
WISCONSIN
ROAD GUIDE
TO
HAUNTED
LOCATIONS

THE
WISCONSIN
ROAD GUIDE
TO
HAUNTED
LOCATIONS

By Chad Lewis & Terry Fisk

Research Publishing Company
A Division of Unexplained Research, LLC

Library of Congress Control Number: 2004114639
ISBN: 0-9762099-1-8

Printed in the United States by Documation

Unexplained Research Publishing Company
A Division of Unexplained Research, LLC
P.O. Box 2173, Eau Claire, WI 54702-2173
Email: info@unexplainedresearch.com
www.unexplainedresearch.com

Cover Design: Terry Fisk
Back Cover Photo: Rob Mattison

DEDICATION

This book is dedicated to my mother, Judy Lewis, for her unwavering love and support.

—Chad

I dedicate this book to my beloved parents, Larry and Lois Fisk, who just celebrated their 50th wedding anniversary.

—Terry

TABLE OF CONTENTS

CONTENTS

7 - Peninsula Wisconsin 187

8 - South Central **Wisconsin**   **207**

9 - Southeastern **Wisconsin**   **229**

CONTENTS

PREFACE

Corrections. Although we have made every effort to be certain that this road guide is reliable and accurate, things inevitably change and errors are made. We would appreciate it when readers contact us so we can revise future editions of the book.

Updates. If you have a paranormal experience at one of these locations, please report it to us. We recommend that you keep a journal, carefully recording dates, times, locations, and what happened.

Additions. Due to lack of space, many locations had to be left out of the book. We do intend to publish a second volume. Please write and let us know of any Wisconsin Locations that you feel should have been included in this travel guide.

Warning. Be respectful of both the living and the dead. Several communities have had problems with people who go to these locations only to party and cause mischief. Cemeteries have been desecrated; private property has been vandalized; grounds have been littered; and buildings have been broken into.

If you do decide to check out any of the locations for yourself, please make sure that you have permission if it is private property, and obey all applicable laws. Under most ordinances, cemeteries are only open from sunrise to sunset.

We will not be held responsible for any persons who decide to conduct their own investigations or for those who choose to break laws.

Disclaimer. The places listed in the book have neither been proved nor disproved to be haunted. Their inclusion in the book is based on the anecdotal reports we have received from numerous individuals. This book is for reference purposes only.

FOREWORD

Road Trip!

Get your motor runnin'.

The mere fact that you've picked up this book means you're already fated. Yes, you need this book.

This is one cool guide. It's utterly unique for Wisconsin, or anywhere for that matter. Buy it. Don't be a schmuck. It's indispensable.

Still not convinced?

When you hear road trip, three things come to mind. Choice of companions. Choice of music. Choice of destination.

Every successful road trip encompasses some measure of all three.

If your companions are a drag, your trip is a drag. 'Nuff said.

Ditto the music. I mean, I like pop divas as much as anybody, but only as eye candy because after more than a few minutes of their heartfelt wailing, it's like suffering the death of a thousand cuts. That won't be copacetic when you're on a lost backroad somewhere hoping to find the Gates of Hell or looking to go *mano a fido* against the Caryville Hellhounds. You need something rousing, something to rearrange your brain. Loud rock anthems or ear blistering hip hop sets the right mood. Something you can yell above while you're speculating on the nature of UFOs, trading tales of Highway 12's phantom hitchhiker, or considering the merits of just the right wood for staking the Mineral Point Vampire. Something that'll cover your own screams when that monster's leering red eyes pop out of the brush or the spirit of a hanged farmer swings into view. Something to serve as a directional finder for the search party when you don't return home.

You need somewhere to go. A destination. That's why you need this book.

This is your road map, your travel companion, your Baedeker, your Bible. Like those books that got you all excited in grade school, you can choose your own adventure. But this is no armchair adventuring. This is the real deal. And it'll give you more ideas than you ever imagined.

Far too many fun trips have gone straight down the one-holer when your so-called knowledgeable but directionally challenged friend proves incapable of finding his or her way out of a ripped gunny sack. I've heard it plenty of times. "We drove for hours in circles, but couldn't find Haunchyville, where the angry midgets live" or "we got lost trying to find that Fifield cemetery where the gnomes throw rocks; where did we turn wrong?" It might make for laughs years down the road, but when it happens, you feel like the world's biggest loser during the non-stop bickering in the car during those frantic hours of wrong turns. It's a bummer to end a friendship because you couldn't find Chicken Alley.

Head out on the highway.

You still have to know how to read a map. But this book takes the guesswork out of finding that obscure narrow lane where Bigfoot roams and werewolves howl. Not only will it get you to an exciting destination painlessly, but it reveals the strange encounters of fellow adventurers, gives clues to landmarks, while also providing some alternate—possibly rational—explanations and history for the haunted locale.

And even if your adventuring goes no further than the comfy armchair in your living room, you can vicariously relish the possibilities Out There through this book.

You can easily visit three haunted Stevens Point bridges in a single afternoon, find Calvin Blood's cemetery, and go trolling for phantom Boy Scouts along Boy Scout Lane, all without too much effort. That's sweet. But if you do visit Highway 66's Bloody Bride Bridge, do it after dark—the bloody bride only comes out at night.

Lookin' for adventure.

I cry the tears of a clown every time I hear people say, "I'm bored. There's nothing to do."

Man—that's sad. You have got to get out more.

Wisconsin is one huge place. And it's one of the weirdest places you'll ever encounter. It just takes some effort on your part. Use the back roads and stay off the freeway. Keep away from chains—eat and buy local. Experienced legend seekers know that not only is the food better, but you're far more likely to pick up chilling tales of blood-soaked madness and gibbering horror in places where the pace is a little slower or they dress a little odder. Every small town or wide spot in the road has something unique to it. Every little cemetery or abandoned building holds some spirit of time past. Open the car windows and you can smell weirdness pouring in from every direction. Inhale.

I admire Chad and Terry tremendously for the hard work they put into this book. They don't just talk the talk—they walk the walk. They've crisscrossed the state to search out bizarre legends, wandered graveyards and decaying schools, investigated weird phenomena from crop circles to UFO abductees to Amery Lutheran

Church ghosts. They've talked to witnesses, police, neighbors, passers-by, business owners, and rooted around in musty old archives and libraries to pull together this chronicle of strange attractions. Nobody works harder than these two researchers and their efforts shine in this book you're holding in your hands.

No matter where you live in this great weird state of ours, there is something nearby just crying out to be explored. Along with this travel companion, you don't need anything more than a camera, really, and the three essentials listed above. Go for an hour, go for a day, go for a week, and you still won't exhaust the possibilities. No one knows better than Terry and Chad how many oddities and really cool stories they had to leave out due to length considerations. Help 'em out—test-drive this guide, spread the word, then pester them for the sequel.

Or whatever comes our way.

Now, be ready. Eyes peeled, senses alert.

If you do have a weird encounter, don't forget to write. Any or all of us would love to hear about your trip. If you don't share your experiences, then we'll never know about them and the world will be a poorer, sadder place for it. Clowns will cry—we wouldn't want that.

As that great songmeister Robert Earl Keen sings, "The road goes on forever, and the party never ends."

Go—discover your own wild.

Richard D. Hendricks
Weird Wisconsin
weird-wi.com
September 2004

ACKNOWLEDGMENTS

We would like to thank Jeannine Stucklen, Chris Belisle, Richard Hendricks, and Tamrah Aeryn for assisting us with the research and production of this book. Thanks to Kathi Rice for the proofreading.

We also want to thank the many people who provided us with cases, directions, and personal accounts.

INTRODUCTIONS

Beneath the tides of sleep and time

Strange fish are moving

—Thomas Wolfe

Often people inquire about why I fly around the world and travel much of the U.S. in search of paranormal phenomena. The answer is quite simple, curiosity. The world is full of events that stretch the boundaries of scientific beliefs. From fish falling from the sky and strange animals dubbed "chupacabras" attacking livestock in Central America to reports of UFOs and spontaneous human combustion. What happens when we die? Are we alone in the universe? These salient questions have baffled humans since the beginning of time. They hint at the very core of what it means to be human.

Nearly all of us have heard someone tell a good ghost story, whether your father was spinning a scary tale around the campfire, or your grandma was sharing her personal experience of seeing a ghost, we have become accustomed to the idea that ghosts do exist. However, the belief in ghosts, also known as apparitions, spirits, spooks, shades, wraiths, specters, phantoms, poltergeists, visions, and nightshades dates back long before us, to the beginning of human existence. Numerous cultures and peoples throughout time have shared the belief that the human soul continues on after the death of the body. Their beliefs included the ability of these spirits to return to this plane and interact with the living.

As you eagerly venture out to the places listed in this book, keep in mind that seeking out spirits was not always considered safe or advisable. The people of ancient Assyria and Babylonia believed there were three classifications of spirits. The first were disembodied souls with devious intentions. The second type of spirits possessed the duality of being half-human and half-demon and were not to be trusted. The last type of spirits were devils that caused plagues and despair among humans. Not quite the type of ghosts many of you are hoping to encounter. However, do not despair, as Greek poet Homer wrote of ghosts and spirits during the 8th century B.C. as "passive and benign spirits." Homer's writings helped to shift the perception of spirits to kinder, more helpful beings.

Wait! Don't run to the car just yet, as it was during the time of Greek philosopher Plato (427-347 B.C.) that the perception of ghosts again shifted back from benign, passive spirits, to spirits that were deemed harmful. Plato warned against the viewing of the souls of those who had not parted this world in pure form. This time period also included the belief that spirits possessed the powers to hurt or kill the living, and those who died too early or of a violent death were considered extremely dangerous. The Romans also followed this trend, and proceeded to bury their loved ones along the roads leading away from their towns and cities. In addition to removing their dead bodies, the Romans performed numerous ceremonies on those who had done evil deeds to dissuade them from returning to the living. Both ancient Rome and Greece participated in the festivals of the dead. The festival lasted several days in which shops would close, temples would shut down, and social activities were postponed. Residents smeared their doors with pitch and chewed whitethorn in order to ward off spirits.

Again do not despair, as during the 1800s the spiritualist movement received marked popularity. The spiritualist movement believed that the soul of the living that passed on with the death of the body could be contacted by those still living. The movement believed that spirits were the same in death as they were in life.

Hold on one more second, as you are still not ready to set out on your adventure. What about your equipment? Many ghost researchers scramble to have the longest list of equipment used in their research. Although I do use a lot of scientific equipment from motion detectors, thermo cameras, night vision, electro magnetic field detectors, video cameras, Geiger counters, and digital recorders, I feel there are only two essential pieces of equipment necessary to conduct your own research. The first is a camera, and the second you are holding in your hands right now. Some of the best ghost research ever conducted was done without modern equipment. A list of equipment needed for a 1930's ghost investigation included a measuring tape, matches and candles, a notebook, and a camera. Do not be discouraged by not having thousands of dollars of equipment that others say you must have. There is no piece of equipment that will replace curiosity and common sense.

Now that you are armed with a sense of adventure and your newly acquired guidebook, you have no excuse not to explore every corner of the state. You can no longer justify spending count-less hours in front of the TV wishing life was more interesting. Why simply watch a ghost movie when you can actually live a ghost movie? Life is too short to waste it. No one on their death-bed wishes their life would have been less exciting. It is up to you to create your own adventure, and this book will give you that nec-essary kick-start. Trust me when I tell you that you will have a dif-ficult time finding more interesting people, places, and stories any-where else in the world. On second thought, do not trust me, find out for yourself, travel the world, take in the sights, sounds, and people, and soak up everything life has to offer, and then decide for yourself.

Good luck on your adventure,

Chad Lewis

The most beautiful thing we can experience is the mysterious. It is the source of all true art and science. He to whom this emotion is a stranger, who can no longer pause to wonder and stand rapt in awe, is as good as dead: his eyes are closed.

—Albert Einstein

Do ghosts exist? To be honest with you, I don't know. The belief in ghosts is ubiquitous, being found in every culture in the world today and throughout history. In this country, the belief is growing rapidly. In 1978, a Gallup Poll found that one in ten people believed in ghosts. By 1990, it had increased to one in three people. Now, a 2003 Harris Poll finds that over half of the public, including 58% of women and 65% of young people 25 to 29, believe in ghosts.

The fact that a majority of people believes in something doesn't mean that it's true. As astronomer Carl Sagan so often said, "Extraordinary claims require extraordinary evidence," to which researcher Budd Hopkins responded, "Extraordinary claims require extraordinary investigations."

Chad and I investigate these extraordinary claims, and we've found that when it comes to the paranormal, most people are firmly rooted at one of two extremes. They are either close-minded believers or close-minded cynics. Chad and I tend to take the middle road. Ours is an agnostic approach of being honest enough to admit that we just don't know for a certainty whether or not ghosts exist. We try not to form our conclusions before gathering and examining the evidence. Emulating philosopher Bertrand Russell's approach, we strive to have an open mind, but not so open that our brains fall out.

We are constantly criticized by cynics who feel we shouldn't even be investigating the paranormal; perhaps they fear that their materialist worldview could be shattered. On the other side, we are also criticized by believers who worry that we might remove some mystery from their lives. I wholeheartedly agree that we all need a sense of wonder. I would much rather live in a huge world full of mystery and uncertainty, than in a world so tiny and simple that we could actually comprehend it. Fortunately, history has shown us that gaining knowledge does not destroy our sense of mystery. There are always new mysteries that come along to replace the old ones. One piece of wisdom that I've learned is that the most meaningful things in life aren't the answers to be found, but it's the mysteries to be lived.

Godspeed on your journey into the unknown, and may you enjoy the thrill and awe of this mysterious world we live in.

Terry Fisk

CENTRAL WISCONSIN

Spiritland Cemetery

Location: Almond, Portage County Almond Township, Wisconsin
Correction: Some sources erroneously list it as being in Plainfield, Wisconsin
AKA: Sometimes spelled as "Spirit Land" (two words)

Directions: From Hwy 39/51 go east on Cty Rd D. Immediately past the intersection of Cty Rd D and Cty Rd BB, the cemetery will be on the right.

Ghost Lore

There are rumors that this is the cemetery where psycho Ed Gein robbed graves, and after his death he was buried here.

Many people believe that Ed Gein's nighttime frolicking and grave robbing have permanently disturbed the dead in the cemetery.

Investigation

This is the classic spooky cemetery with a definite Halloween atmosphere to it. Even the name seems appropriate.

Ed Gein was not buried here. He was interred at the Plainfield Cemetery in Plainfield, Wisconsin; however, this cemetery was apparently the site of at least one grave robbery by Gein.

After his arrest, Gein had confessed to a series of unreported grave robberies. The authorities were later able to confirm this by exhuming three of the graves. In one, the body was mutilated; in the second, the body was missing; and in the third, the body was intact, but the casket showed evidence of tampering.

History

According to local historians, the cemetery got its name because Dewit McLaughlin, one of Almond's early settlers, lost his wife, and she was buried in this cemetery. Mr. McLaughlin would regularly visit his wife's grave, and it is said that her spirit used to appear to him.

Charlotte Mills Bridge

Location: Christie, Clark County, Wisconsin

Directions: From Hwy 10 in Neillsville take Cty Rd 73 north to Christie, turn left on Cty Rd H. The bridge is about a mile down the road.

Ghost Lore

Almost a hundred years ago, in the town of Christie, Wisconsin, a woman named Charlotte Mills took her life near the bridge that crosses the Black River. Since then, many people believe that on chilly October nights, her ghost walks the bridge and mourns the death of her sons who died during the month of October.

History

Charlotte A. Raymond was born in Manlius, New York, in 1840. When she was three, her parents, Luther Raymond and Julia Ann Loomis, moved the family to Wisconsin, locating in the vicinity of Waukesha. Two years later they moved to Fond du Lac County, securing a tract of wild land, from which Luther developed a farm. Years later, Charlotte married a Mr. Ransom and they had two sons: Fay (b. 1859) and Benjamin (b. 1862). After her husband died, she married Calvin John Mills in 1866. Four years later they moved to Christie, Wisconsin and this marriage produced a third son, Claude Lee Mills, who was born in 1877.

In 1883, her father Luther died.

In the spring of 1899, her son Fay bade his parents farewell and moved away from Wisconsin, traveling to South Dakota, Montana, California, and finally to Alaska in search of gold. Then one day, Charlotte received the sad news that her son had drowned near Labarge, Alaska on October 12th, 1901 on the steamer Goddard ten miles from shore, during a gale.

One year later, she received more sad news. Her second son Benjamin had died on October 2nd, 1902 in Mackay, Idaho.

In 1905, her husband Calvin John Mills died very suddenly of heart failure while at their home at Christie. After his death, Charlotte fell into a severe depression and expressed to her son Claude her feelings that her life was pointless, full of misfortune, and not worth living.

On October 4, 1907, Charlotte, who was probably dwelling on thoughts about her two sons who had died during the month of October, told her son Claude that she was going to visit one of her friends. Because she would often spend the night at the friend's house, it was not unexpected when she did not return that evening. However, after she was gone for two days, Claude became concerned and went to look for her. When she was not found at the

5

neighbor's house, Claude searched near the Black River finding her footprints, then her shawl, and finally her body floating in shallow water near the shore. Later, he found that, before going to her death, his mother had carefully laid out on her bed the clothes that she wanted to be buried in.

Investigation

On October 31st, a hunter from Iowa was returning home when he encountered a ghostly mist while crossing the bridge. In the months following Charlotte's death, as many as eight farmers reported seeing nebulous mists and strange lights hovering over the bridge. They were convinced that it was the spirit of Charlotte Mills. On one occasion, a farmer's horse could also see the spectral figure and refused to cross the bridge.

It should be noted that this is not the original bridge from Charlotte Mills' time. It has since been replaced twice.

Charlotte and John Calvin Mills are buried in the Neillsville
Cemetery

Clark's True Value Hardware

Location: Plainfield, Waushara County, Wisconsin
Address: 111 S. Main St., Plainfield, WI 54966-8921
Phone: (715) 335-4451

Directions: From Hwy 39/51 take State Hwy 73 east into Plainfield. State Hwy 73 becomes E North St. The store is on the southeast corner of the intersection of E North St and S Main St.

Ghost Lore

One of the former owners of the store was a victim of serial killer Ed Gein. Employees and customers report seeing apparitions of her carrying order forms and talking about anti-freeze.

Investigation

On November 16, 1957, 58-year-old Bernice Worden disappeared from her Plainfield hardware store. There was blood on the floor, with a trail of it leading out the back door. Worden's son Frank, who was the sheriff's deputy, recalled that on the day before she disappeared, Gein mentioned that he needed anti-freeze. Authorities found a sales receipt for anti-freeze inside the store. He also learned that Gein had been spotted in town on the day of his mother's disappearance. So Frank Worden and the sheriff went out to the Gein farm to question Ed.

In a shed, behind Gein's house, they found, to their horror, the headless body of Bernice Worden hung from the rafters "enviscerated and dressed like a deer," as one newspaper put it. In the house, they found her heart in a saucepan, on the stove. Her head had been turned into a macabre ornament, and her other organs were found nearby in a box.

Note: *If you visit the store and make a purchase, that's fine. But we do not recommend that you inquire about Ed Gein or the murders. The local townspeople are understandably sensitive about the subject and would prefer to put it behind them, so please be respectful.*

8

Ed Gein Property

Location: Plainfield, Waushara County, Wisconsin

Directions: From Hwy 39/51 in Plainfield go west on State Hwy 73, turn left on Cty Rd KK, turn right on Archer Ave. The Gein property is on the southwest corner of the intersection of Archer Ave and 2nd Ave. There is a chain across the driveway.

Ghost Lore

The property where Ed Gein's house once stood is haunted. People have heard strange noises in the woods and have seen unexplained lights.

Investigation

Even before his arrest, many of the local youths believed that

Gein's house was haunted. In fact, Gein used to babysit children and tell them that his house was haunted. After his arrest, Ed Gein was determined to be mentally unfit for trial and was committed to the Central State Hospital in Waupun, Wisconsin. On the morning of March 20, 1958, somebody deliberately set fire to his house, and firefighters were unable to prevent it from being razed. All that remains today is an empty lot that has become overgrown with brush. The driveway is closed off with a chain.

Note: *This land is privately owned and posted. You can view the property from the road, but do not trespass.*

Plainfield Cemetery

Location: Plainfield, Waushara County, Wisconsin

Directions: From Hwy 39/51 go east on Hwy 73. The immediate first left turn is 5th Ave. Follow this road around the corner until you see the cemetery on the right.

Ghost Lore

Ironically, serial killer Ed Gein is buried in the same cemetery where he used to rob graves. He is laid to rest not far from some of his victims.

The cemetery is rumored to be haunted and full of restless spirits.

Investigation

After a long bout with cancer, Ed Gein died in a mental hospital on

11

July 26, 1984, at the age of 77 and was buried in the Plainfield Cemetery next to his parents and brother. His grave is not far from the graves that he had robbed years earlier. One of his victims, Bernice Worden, was buried just a few feet from his grave.

On June 15, 2000, thieves stole Gein's 150-pound headstone. It was recovered a year later. Police retrieved it from a Seattle rock band promoter who was selling rubbings from the stone for $50.00 each on his website. The authorities were concerned that the marker would be stolen again if returned to the cemetery, so it currently resides in a Wautoma museum.

People steal dirt from the grave to either sell
or keep as a souvenir

Black Bridge

Location: Stevens Point, Portage County, Wisconsin
AKA: Blackbridge

Directions: From Hwy 10 in Stevens Point (on the east side of the Wisconsin River), turn south on Division St, turn right on Wisconsin St, drive to the dead end. From there you can view both the bridge and the mill.

Ghost Lore

A worker was accidentally killed in the mill near the Black Bridge in Stevens Point. It is rumored that a ghost can be seen on the Black Bridge searching for its lover who died in an accident at the nearby mill.

Investigation

It is likely accidental deaths have occurred at the mill; however, we do not yet have any documented cases.

Black Bridge is the train trestle that crosses the Wisconsin River just below the Point Dam in Stevens Point. Nearby, on the east side of the river, is the mill. We are currently searching for witnesses who have had first-hand experiences.

The mill near the Black Bridge

Blood Cemetery

Location: Stevens Point, Portage County, Wisconsin
AKA: Woodville Cemetery or Linwood Town Cemetery

Directions: From Hwy 10 in Stevens Point (on the west side of the Wisconsin River) turn on W Clark St, which becomes Cty Rd P, turn left on Mill Creek Dr, turn left on W River Dr, turn right on Cemetery Rd. The cemetery is on the immediate right.

Ghost Lore

- One story is that Calvin Blood hanged himself in a tree in the cemetery. According to other versions, it was another member of the Blood family member who committed suicide. Others claim the hanging occurred in the woods near Boy Scout Lane.

- Another story about Calvin Blood is that he was a deserter

15

during the Civil War. His battalion tracked him down to Stevens Point and hanged him in the tree that currently overlooks his grave.

- A different account is that Calvin Blood was a young boy who died from a rare blood disease and was buried under the tree in the cemetery.

- People have reported a variety of strange experiences here. Most frequent is that the tree near the grave will bleed actual drops of blood.

- It is also commonly reported that people encounter mechanical problems with their vehicles. Their car won't start, it overheats, or the interior lights turn on and off.

- People have been chased by mysterious blue lights. Strong winds blow inside the cemetery, but not outside it. Then there's that tree by the grave that will bleed actual drops of blood.

The Dare: There is a crooked tree outside the cemetery. If you touch it, you will be cursed.

Investigation

Calvin Blood was born October 9, 1825, serviced in the Wisconsin Infantry during the Civil War, was wounded on April 2, 1865, married Sarah Barden, and, in the end, died of consumption on February 1, 1907, at the ripe old age of 81. There were no suicides, no lynchings, and no rare blood diseases.

This cemetery is in bad condition due to vandalism. Most of the stones are gone and the remaining stones are unreadable with two exceptions. Both of which are new. One is a single grave marker which reads Hosea FULLER 1820-1900. The other marker is a group marker which contains the names of six Civil War veterans.

The names and inscriptions are as follows:

Calvin BLOOD PVT Co A 5 WI Infantry Civil War Oct 9, 1825–Feb 1, 1907

Henry HUTCHINS PVT Co I 18 WI Infantry Civil War 1812–1896

William COLBY PVT Co E 3 WI Infantry Civil War Dec 6, 1832 –Mar 18, 1915

Tola LAWSON PVT Co E 18 WI Infantry Civil War 1840–1882

Jacob COLEMAN U S Army Civil War

Enos STODDARD PVT Co D 5 WI Infantry Civil War May 2, 1833–Aug 18, 1896

Note: *The cemetery has had an unfortunate history of teenage beer parties and vandalism. In fact, Calvin Blood's original tombstone was stolen. Currently the cemetery is locked and trespassing is prohibited. We recommend that you view it only from the fence.*

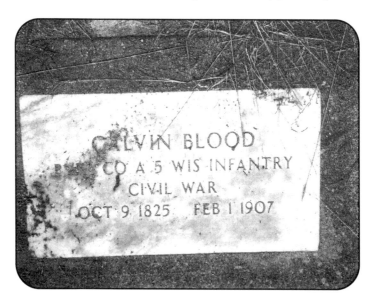

Bloody Bride Bridge

Location: Stevens Point, Portage County, Wisconsin

Directions: From Stevens Point take State Hwy 66 northeast to Jordan. The bridge crosses the Plover River less than half a mile east of Jordan.

Ghost Lore

A young bride was killed on her wedding night in an auto accident on "Bloody Bride Road."

While driving down this road, a police officer witnessed an apparition of the young bride standing in the middle of the road. Unable to stop in time, his vehicle struck the figure. He stopped his car and looked back to see if her body was still laying on the road and was startled to find the Bloody Bride sitting in the backseat of his squad car.

Dare #1: If you drive down Bloody Bride Road, you will see the Bloody Bride standing on the side of the road, still wearing her wedding gown.

Dare #2: If you park your car on the Bloody Bride Bridge after midnight and look in your rearview mirror, you will see both the groom and the Bloody Bride sitting in the backseat of your car.

Investigation

"Bloody Bride Road" is actually Highway 66. Nobody at the Stevens Point Police Department has any recollection of a bride ever having been killed on this road.

According to Stevens Point Police Department, this incident with the police officer never happened. If an accident did take place on Highway 66, it would have been investigated by the sheriff's department. We spoke with several employees of the sheriff's department who had no memory of a girl dying on Highway 66.

Boy Scout Lane

Location: Stevens Point, Portage County, Wisconsin
Corrections: Some sources erroneously spell it as Boyscouts Lane

Directions: From Hwy 10 in Stevens Point (on the west side of the Wisconsin River) turn on W Clark St, which becomes Cty Rd P, turn left on Mill Creek Dr, turn left on W River Dr, turn left on Boy Scout Ln, which is a dead end.

Ghost Lore

The road got its name because of a tragic event that occurred here.

One version is that a troop of Boy Scouts on a camping trip were murdered by their bus driver on this isolated road.

Another version of the story is that a Boy Scout troop mysteriously disappeared on this road and was never seen again.

A third story is that a troop of Boy Scouts were camping here and some of them were wandering around at night and accidentally dropped a lantern resulting in a forest fire that killed the rest of the troop.

The road is rumored to be haunted by dead Boy Scouts. After dark a swinging light, that appears to be a lantern carried by somebody, perhaps a Boy Scout, has been seen on the road. Supposedly, the light is carried by the ghosts of the Scouts who are searching for their troop that they accidentally killed in a fire.

Investigation

There is no evidence of missing persons or a mass murder or a tragic fire. The road got its name because at one time the Boy Scouts owned the land along the road and had intentions of building a Boy Scout camp.

We did speak with one individual who provided a firsthand account of having seen the moving light on the road.

Old Swenson

Location: Stevens Point, Portage County, Linwood Township, Wisconsin

AKA: Old Swanson

Directions: From Hwy 10 in Stevens Point (on the west side of the Wisconsin River) turn on W Clark St, which becomes Cty Rd P, turn right on Cty Rd I I.

Ghost Lore

While traveling down the rural country road in Linwood Township, motorists will unexpectedly encounter the ghost of a man searching for the grave of his wife. In the ghost's hand are flowers intended for his wife. The ghost is sometimes reported to be floating, as he is missing his legs.

Investigation

We found several stories about this case.

- A driver was traveling along County Road I I when a man on the side of the road flagged him down. The man was carrying flowers and asked the driver if he knew where his wife was buried. The driver, who was from out of town, told the man that he could not help him and drove off. However, upon driving off, the driver noticed that the man had no legs and was floating in midair.

- Many residents report that the ghost is Swenson (or Swanson in some versions) who worked for Soo Line in the early 1900s and was killed in a railroad accident that severed both of his legs just above the knees.

- According to one story, shortly after Swenson died, his wife died. Her parents never liked Old Swenson so they decided to bury their daughter in a different cemetery instead of next to her deceased husband.

- Another version is that Swenson initially survived the accident, and his wife died while he was still in the hospital. Her family, opposed to the marriage, buried her without telling him where her grave was. Eventually he died from his injuries and was buried in a different location.

- It is believed that Old Swenson spends his time hopelessly searching for the grave of his beloved wife. He is usually described as being short and dressed in white with a forlorn look on his face.

- There are no railroad tracks or cemeteries on County Road I I. We did not experience the ghost of Swenson during our investigation.

- We have not yet found any information on the death of Old Swenson.

Red Bridge

Location: Stevens Point, Portage County, Wisconsin
AKA: Redbridge

Directions: From Hwy 66 in Stevens Point, take 2nd St N north, it becomes N 2nd Dr, turn left on Casimir Rd, turn left on Walkush Rd, stop at the red bridge.

Ghost Lore

The bridge is rumored to be haunted.

The Dare: If you park your car on the bridge at midnight and shut off your headlights, the ghost of a woman will appear and walk across the bridge.

Investigation

The Red Bridge is west of Casimir and crosses over the backwaters of the Wisconsin River.

We received a report from eyewitnesses who saw not one, but three ghosts on the bridge. It appeared to be a family of ghosts that included the woman. The witnesses saw the car ahead of them actually pass right through the ghostly figures. Later, they found their clean car to be covered with dusty handprints.

Hotel Mead

Location: Wisconsin Rapids, Wood County, Wisconsin
Address: 451 E. Grand Ave., Wisconsin Rapids, WI 54494-4853
Phone: (715) 842-0988
Reservations: (800) THE-MEAD or (800) 843-6323
TDD: (715) 422-7069
Fax: (715) 422-7064
Email: info@hotelmead.com

Ghost Lore

It is reported that the Shanghai room in the basement is haunted. It is rumored that sometime during the 1950s (1953?) the room was used as a bar, and a female bartender was stabbed to death there.

• The room has a distinct scent of blood (from a distance of 20 feet).

- Lights flicker.

- Doors shut by themselves.

- The room is unusually cold.

Investigation

The Hotel Mead is an upscale establishment that does not allow employees to speak with reporters or investigators. However, several employees were willing to speak with us on the condition of anonymity.

We spoke with two young employees that have been working there for about a year. Both of the ladies had heard the stories of the haunting, but neither of them had any personal experience within the room. A custodian that we interviewed had never heard of the place being haunted. Another employee working in the restaurant also had no knowledge of the room reportedly being haunted.

The last employee we spoke with has worked at the hotel for over 20 years and had never heard the story of it being haunted or of a woman being killed there.

During a subsequent visit we did speak with a desk clerk who acknowledged that he was aware of the haunting activities in the Shanghai room. He knew about the flickering lights but had not experienced anything personally. He recommended that we speak with a particular bartender. Upon questioning the bartender, he nervously acknowledged the fact that the room was haunted, but when pressed for further details, he simply turned his back to us and refused to discuss the matter.

The smell of the blood could be explained by the fact that the meat locker and butchering room were located next to the Shanghai room, which is now used for a liquor storage room. The coldness of the room could be because it is located in the basement.

Clara Bates, a bar owner in the nearby city of Kellner, was murdered in 1952. That case is detailed in the books *The Tangled Web* by John M. Potter and *Please Pass the Roses* by Colleen Kohler Kanieski. This case could have been a possible source for the rumor at the Hotel Mead.

We have learned that in the '60s (not the '50s), a female employee of the Mead was killed, supposedly at an after-hours party. Our investigation into the nature of this death and the possible haunting activity is ongoing.

CHIPPEWA VALLEY WISCONSIN

Green-eyes Bridge

Location: Augusta, Eau Claire County, Bridge Creek
Township, Wisconsin
AKA: Troubled Waters Bridge

Directions: From Augusta, take Cty Rd G north. After crossing the Eau Claire River, turn left into the parking area. The
bridge will be to the east.

Ghost Lore

Several years ago, a resident of Augusta, Wisconsin, murdered his
family then committed suicide by hanging himself on the bridge
over the Eau Claire River. His ghost has haunted the bridge for
nearly 100 years. According to another version of the story, the suicide happened during the Depression. At night, a silhouette of the
murderer's body can be seen hanging from the girders of the

bridge. According to other accounts, the body is seen hanging off the side of the bridge.

Despite the discrepancies over when and where the death occurred, most stories are consistent in averring that after dark, the glowing green eyes of the murderer can be seen on or near the bridge.

Investigation

- We have been unable to verify the homicide/suicide story.

- No silhouette was observed by investigators.

- We did manage to capture the possible cause of the mysterious glowing "green eyes" and have it analyzed by entomologist Paula K. Kleintjes, Ph.D. at the University of Wisconsin–Eau Claire. She determined that the "green eyes" were simply fire-fly larvae—better known as "glow worms." Some witnesses discount this, claiming to have seen the green eyes in the winter when there would be no insects.

- We spoke with someone who reported that in 1994 or 1995 she had stayed in a cabin, near the bridge, with some friends. After driving into Augusta for supplies, they returned to the cabin and found ropes tied into nooses and a mysterious shadow draped across the piano. They hastily left without taking time to retrieve their gear, and they never returned.

Caryville Cemetery

Location: Elk Mound, Dunn County, Spring Brook Township, Wisconsin
The Official Name: The Sand Hill Cemetery

Directions: From Clairemont Ave in Eau Claire, take Cty Rd E west, turn left on 890th St, turn right on 260th Ave, turn left on 240th Ave. The cemetery is on the left.

Ghost Lore

- The graveyard was featured on *Unsolved Mysteries* a few years ago, and they were able to document the ghostly activities in the cemetery.

- The ghosts of children have been observed running in the field next to the cemetery.

- Some have reported seeing the ghosts of the children playing in the cemetery. The ghosts are even alleged to approach people and speak to them.

- A tall, dark, shadowy figure has been seen in the graveyard. This could be "Blackie," the shadowy demon reported at both the Caryville schoolhouse and the Meridean boat landing.

- Growling sounds have been reported and are believed to be the hellhounds.

- Things usually happen in the graveyard after midnight and especially on Halloween.

- Ouija boards go out of control in the cemetery.

The Dare: There is a neglected cemetery farther back in the woods. If you curse or spit on one of those graves, a boxer (i.e., a pugilist, not a dog) will appear.

Investigation

- It is doubtful that the cemetery was ever featured on *Unsolved Mysteries.*

- We were unable to locate a secondary cemetery in the woods, and the owner of the land denies its existence.

- Investigators have not observed anything paranormal.

Caryville Church

Location: Elk Mound, Dunn County, Spring Brook Township, Wisconsin
Official Name: Spring Brook Lutheran Church

Directions: From Clairemont Ave in Eau Claire, take Cty Rd E west, turn left on Cty Rd H, turn right on 930th Ave. The church will be on the right.

Ghost Lore

The church was built by a priest named "Jacob" who put so much time and effort in its construction that he was willing to die for it. About 30 years ago, some investors came to Caryville and wanted to demolish both the church and the Caryville schoolhouse across the road and construct new ones. The minister became so enraged that he removed the stairs from the church and hung himself in the belfry. Later the townspeople spotted his body hanged in the bell tower.

Paranormal events have occurred ever since the suicide of the clergyman. People have seen the ghost of the priest hanging inside the bell tower.

Investigation

- The stories about a priest are obviously false, since this is a Lutheran church, and only Catholic and Episcopalian churches have priests; Lutheran churches have ministers.

- Local residents and church members refute the story that a clergyman hanged himself in the belfry of the church.

- The rumors of haunting activity have been around for only 5-10 years—not 30 years.

- It is doubtful that anybody has seen an apparition of a body hanging in the belfry, since the story about the suicide is untrue.

- According to local residents and members of the church, nothing paranormal has ever occurred at the church or the schoolhouse.

Note: *The congregation has had problems with people breaking and entering and vandalizing the church. Please respect them, and do not trespass.*

Caryville Schoolhouse

Location: Elk Mound, Dunn County, Spring Brook Township, Wisconsin
Official Name: Fosbrook School

Directions: From Clairemont Ave in Eau Claire, take Cty Rd E west, turn left on Cty Rd H, turn right on 930th Ave. The schoolhouse will be on the left.

Ghost Lore

- There was a young boy who attended school there who died in his desk under mysterious circumstances.

- A second version of the story is that on a chilly, winter day, a little boy refused to go home to his drunken, abusive father, and hid in the schoolhouse. The next morning, the teacher found his frozen little corpse sitting at his desk.

- A third version is that a preacher killed all the school children, then hanged himself in the belfry.

- Many creepy events have occurred in the schoolhouse.

- In the last window, on the right-side of the schoolhouse, a pair of black eyes has been spotted staring out.

- A girl was raped by a ghost inside the schoolhouse. Later blood was found splattered on the walls.

- The school grounds are haunted by "Blackie," a shadowy demon who will sometimes shake your vehicle when you are parked near the school. This may be the same shadowy creature reported to have been seen at both the Caryville Cemetery and Meridean boat landing.

- A familiar in the form of a three-legged, one-eyed, black cat guards the school and will stare at you with its evil eye if you approach the building.

- A rope with a noose hangs in the belfry.

- People report feeling a mysterious gust of air inside the school.

The Dare: If you sit in the desk that the young boy died in, you will feel something strange pass through your body.

Investigation

- There was indeed a seven-year-old boy, David James Grohn (born May 27, 1949), who died while attending the school. He passed away at 11:45 p.m. on September 24, 1957, not during a cold winter day. His death occurred at Luther Hospital in Eau Claire, not while sitting in his desk at school. An autopsy determined the cause of death to be bulbar poliomyelitis (i.e., polio), and the examining physician, C.H. Falstad, M.D., found nothing mysterious or unexpected about his death. Furthermore, there is no reason to believe that his father was

37

ever abusive to him.

- There is no evidence that a preacher ever committed murder or suicide in the school.

- Nothing paranormal has been substantiated.

- The story of a girl being raped by a ghost is unsubstantiated. There is no evidence of any blood stains on the walls.

- The existence of the cat is possible, but we have not observed it.

- We spoke with a witness who claimed to have observed the noose, but we have not seen it for ourselves.

- This witness also claimed to have felt a mysterious gust of air inside the school.

- It is doubtful that anybody would know precisely which desk young David Grohn used to sit in, since it was almost 50 years ago. Investigators found that sitting in each of the desks resulted in nothing out of the ordinary.

Note: The schoolhouse has had a problem with trespassing. Please be warned that it is under constant surveillance and trespasser will be arrested and fined.

Hellhounds of Meridean

Location: Elk Mound, Dunn County, Spring Brook Township, Wisconsin
Official Name: Meridean Boat Landing
Corrections: Some sources erroneously spell Meridean as "Meridian" or "Maridean." Other sources erroneously refer to the Chippewa River as the "Meridian" River.

Directions: From Clairemont Ave in Eau Claire, take Cty Rd E west, turn left on Cty Rd H, turn right on 930th Ave, turn right on 230th Ave, turn right on 240th Ave. The boat landing will be on the left.

Ghost Lore

- The ghost of a young girl named "Mary Dean" haunts the island and boat landing where she had committed suicide.

- Shortly after the death of Mary Dean, three ferries mysteriously disappeared in that area, resulting in the ferry crossing being closed down.

- Several teens have drowned while swimming at the boat landing. Their deaths have been ruled as suicides.

- At one time there was a sanitarium on the island run by a doctor who owned several dogs. These dogs haunt the area as "hellhounds," in other words, as black phantom dogs with red glowing eyes.

- Another story is that the dogs viciously killed their owner's child.

- About 50 years ago, two youths, who were parked in their pickup truck at the boat landing, were killed by some type of beast. Their bodies were never recovered. The authorities later found their empty truck, which was splattered with blood mingled with hairs from some unknown type of creature.

- The ghost of Mary Dean has been spotted near the boat landing.

- After dark, some people have heard the howling and gnarling of the hellhounds, others have seen the glowing red eyes of the beasts in the woods near the boat landing, and a few have actually seen the hellhounds running down the Caryville Road.

- Other witnesses have reported hearing movement and screams come from the nearby woods at night and seeing a dark shadowy figure dart across the road. Could this be "Blackie," the demonic figure reported at both the Caryville schoolhouse and cemetery?

- According to an eyewitness, on one dark night there was a bonfire and a huge chair (similar to the statue at the Lincoln Memorial, only on stilts) across the road from the boat landing. Three pairs of glowing red eyes could also be seen in the woods nearby.

The Dare: If you park your car near the boat landing, at the bottom of the hill below the Caryville Cemetery, and shut off your headlights, the hellhounds will appear.

Investigation

- During the lumbering days, there was a town named Meridean on the island. What is today used as a boat landing was at one time a ferry crossing where people traversed the Chippewa River to the island.

- Historians have uncovered a number of stories about how Meridean got its name. All of them make reference to a girl named "Mary Dean." The favored story is that a Mrs. Dean and her charming, young daughter Mary were traveling on the Chippewa River by steamboat. Mary won the hearts of many of the passengers during the journey. She suddenly became ill and was taken ashore. She died and was buried under a tree. The area was then named "Meridean" to commemorate her.

- Although there was once a thriving lumber town on the island, we have been unable to confirm the historicity of a doctor alleged to have had a sanitarium and dogs. According to local historian Dick Feeney, there never was a sanitarium on the island.

- We have been unable to find any documentation verifying the alleged disappearances of the ferries.

- While it is certainly possible that swimmers have drowned there, we know of no documented cases.

- We have found no evidence to confirm the story about the deaths of two people in a pickup truck.

- Our investigative team did hear a strange animal-like sound that emanated from the island. The sound was unidentifiable and not comparable to any known animal sounds.

- We did interview the eyewitness who saw the huge chair and

41

glowing red eyes. It is possible that the "chair" was actually a deer stand, as this area is very popular with hunters.

- The Meridean boat landing and island are popular places for camping and teen parties, so it's not uncommon for there to be bonfires in this area. This could also account for the sounds of screams.

Phantom Cars of Caryville Road

Location: Elk Mound, Dunn County, Spring Brook Township, Wisconsin
Official Name: The road is 240th Avenue

Directions: From Clairemont Ave in Eau Claire, take Cty Rd E west, turn left on Cty Rd H, turn right on 930th Ave, turn right on 230th Ave, turn right on 240th Ave. The bridge is on this road before you get to the boat landing.

Ghost Lore

Several years ago a young girl driving home from prom was killed when her red car veered off the bridge.

Another version of the story is that it was a beautiful prom queen named "Jenny" who lost her life on the bridge. On prom night twenty years ago, Jenny was driving home after a night of partying. She was drunk, and lost control of her pickup truck resulting in a fatal accident at the bridge.

- Headlights, taillights, and inside lights will sometimes fail to function on your car.

- The interior of your car will become ice cold, no matter how high you turn up the heat.

- The old red car (in other versions it is a pickup truck) of the girl killed on prom night can be seen still driving the road.

- An odometer check from county road H to the bridge reveals a time/space warp. The distance from the bridge to H is longer than the distance measured from H to the bridge.

- The headlights of phantom cars will appear and disappear on the road nearby.

- Phantom cars will chase you or play chicken with you as you drive down the road.

The Dare: It is said that if you look into the water while going over the bridge, you might catch a glimpse of her headlights shining through the dark churning water.

Investigation

- According to longtime residents, nobody, least of all a prom queen, was ever killed in a car accident at the bridge.

- An odometer check revealed that the distance to and from the bridge is 1.9 miles both ways.

- No phantom cars or headlights were observed.

- No headlights were observed in the water near the bridge.

Sheeley House

Location: Chippewa Falls, Chippewa County, Wisconsin
Proper Name: James Sheeley House Restaurant
AKA: The James Sheeley House or Sheeley House & Saloon
Address: 236 W. River St., Chippewa Falls, WI 54729-2353
Phone: (715) 726-0561

Ghost Lore

Supposedly the Sheeley House was a boarding house when it was first built, but now is a saloon/restaurant with frequent haunting activity.

- The sound of footsteps can be heard walking up and down the stairs at night after closing hours.

- A mural of roses on the wall that keeps bleeding through every time it's painted over.

- An employee was locked in a freezer by an unseen entity.

History

1868 – Carl Hering purchased the property for his family and started Hering's carriage and blacksmith shop out of the back of his property.

1884 – John Paul purchased the Hering place. Mr. Paul did major reconstruction turning the property into the Paul House with a saloon on the first floor, living quarters, a large kitchen, and some second floor sleeping rooms.

1905 – James Sheeley and his wife Kate purchased the property. James tended the bar while Kate and their three children, Anna, William, and Howard were responsible for cooking the meals and maintaining the rooms.

1913 – James Sheeley died. Kate continued to serve meals and rent out rooms; however, the saloon was leased out.

1934 – Kate died due to complications from her fall down the Sheeley house stairs. Anna Sheeley continued to rent rooms but stopped serving food at the house.

1967 – The saloon closed, but boarding rooms were still available to rent.

1981 – Anna left her home of 76 years, when she could no longer live on her own.

1991 – Anna died at the Golden Age Home.

The house fell into disarray and was painstakingly renovated, using photographs of the original place as guides.

2001– Jim Bloms, the current owner purchased the Sheeley House. The first floor is still the saloon, the second floor is mainly used for dining, and the third floor is used for overfill dining and storage.

Investigation

While the place was being renovated, a very large, heavy piece of equipment was left overnight in the saloon. When the worker came back in the morning, the machine had been moved, although no one had been in the building.

Several employees have reported hearing footsteps on the stairs, and when they investigated, there was no one there.

The wait staff reported that numerous spoons fell from thin air and landed on the floor in the dining room.

When Jim Bloms was refinishing the steps on the staircase, he noticed large men's footsteps that appeared on the top two steps. Mr. Bloms was certain no one had walked on the staircase during that time. The steps now are carpeted; however, the footsteps still remain buried beneath the carpet.

Mr. Bloms' daughter also had a recent encounter while in the dining room. She believed that she heard someone say her name, yet she was unable to trace where it came from.

Mr. Blom was also painting over a mural on the second floor and the roses from that mural would keep bleeding through regardless of what they did to prevent it. It should be noted that the mural was a recent painting and Mr. Blom believes that the type of paint used was responsible for the bleeding.

In the saloon, located in the middle of the walls is a stencil border of intricate printed S's. While the workers assured the owner that all the S's were there when they finished, one S is now missing from the border.

One former employee reported being locked in the freezer. The employee thought his fellow employees were playing a joke on him. After one-half hour, he was able to pick the lock and escape. He could not find any cause for the incident.

Alex of Fire Station 10

Location: Eau Claire, Eau Claire County, Wisconsin
Address: 559 N. Hastings Way, Eau Claire, WI 54703-3438
Phone: (715) 839-0996

Ghost Lore

The fire station is haunted by "Alex," a former firefighter who died several years ago.

Investigation

Alex Arnie Blum (b. August 3, 1903) was a firefighter who worked at Fire Station No. 10. He died on May 11, 1981 of arteriosclerotic heart disease at the age of 77 and was buried in the Scandinavian Lutheran Cemetery in Eau Claire.

- The haunting activity began shortly after Alex Blum passed away.

- Apparitions of "Alex" have been seen by about 80 percent of the firefighters who work there.

- Pots and pans have flown off the wall in the station.

- Heavy metal doors have opened and closed by themselves.

- An electrician was doing electrical work at the station, and while standing on a ladder, he felt a hand tap him on his shoulder. Turning his head, he caught a glimpse of a hand that quickly vanished. The electrician rushed out of the station leaving his tools behind and never even returned for them.

Banbury Place

Location: Eau Claire, Eau Claire County, Wisconsin
Address: 800 Wisconsin St., Eau Claire, WI 54703-3588
Phone: (715) 836-6828

Ghost Lore

- Banbury Place consists of a labyrinth of 13 old buildings that used to be a rubber factory.

- In building number 13, an electrician was accidentally electrocuted while working after hours on an air-conditioning unit. His charred body wasn't discovered until the following week.

- There was a major fire in one of the buildings resulting in a fatality.

- Building number 4 is chained shut with a huge metal chain, and the interior is overrun with rats.

- There is a maze of underground tunnels that connect the buildings. Occasionally homeless people will utilize them as a makeshift domicile.

- One of the buildings is a former shoe factory. For some unknown reason it was shut down in mid-production, and the equipment and materials were abandoned. Partially assembled shoes, pieces of rubber, and open bottles of glue are still sitting there as if the workers just suddenly evacuated the building in the middle of production. One rumor is that the company moved to Chippewa Falls and is now the Red Wing shoe company.

- Ever since the person was killed in building 13, people have heard strange sounds such as moans, screams, and the hum of an old air conditioning unit. This building is alleged to be the scariest.

- In building 4, people have sensed an eerie presence.

- People have reported seeing strange figures and shadows down in the tunnels.

Investigation

- Banbury Place used to be the Uniroyal plant where they manufactured tires. There probably were workers who were accidentally killed by the machinery.

- Apparently, there was a tenant who was growing marijuana plants and died of an accidental electrocution while attempting to hook up an air conditioner for temperature control. His body was not found for two weeks afterward.

- We have found no evidence of a major fire resulting in a fatality.

- We are not aware of a Red Wing shoe factory in Chippewa

Falls, but there is a Mason Shoes factory there. Apparently there never was a shoe factory in Banbury Place.

- When we were hosting *The Unexplained* radio talk show from WOLF 108 FM studios in Banbury Place, one of the disk jockeys reported seeing a ghost. She was working alone in the studio with the outside door locked. Through the studio window she glimpsed a man wearing a red shirt walking down the hallway. Later she looked up and saw him standing on the other side of the window staring at her. Suddenly, he walked through the window and wall, came toward her, and passed through her body. She reported feeling a sensation of hot and cold, but was otherwise unharmed.

The Stones Throw

Location: Eau Claire, Eau Claire County, Wisconsin
Address: 304 Eau Claire St., Eau Claire, WI 54701-3645
Phone: (715) 552-5882

Ghost Lore

Supposedly a man hanged himself there in the early 1900s, and ever since the bar/restaurant in the basement has been haunted.

Investigation

We have been unable to verify the alleged suicide, but virtually everyone who has worked there has had a paranormal experience.

- Sounds of footsteps in the old kitchen hallways.

- Beer bottles mysterious break or fly across the room.

- Objects are misplaced.

- Doors open and close on their own.

- On one occasion, after the customers had left and the bar had closed, the bartender was getting ready to lock up and jokingly shouted, "Okay, everybody out!" At that moment, a previously unnoticed figure stood up from his chair, shook out his jacket, and walked to the front door where he instantly vanished into thin air. The bartender left and never returned to his job.

Mary of Elk Lake Dam

Location: Elk Creek, Dunn County, Wisconsin

Directions: From Clairemont Ave in Eau Claire, take Cty Rd E west to Elk Creek, turn right just before the bridge. Do not confuse this Elk Creek with the one in Trempealeau County.

Ghost Lore

A young woman, hitchhiking across the state of Wisconsin, was murdered near Elk Lake Dam, and her ghost haunts the area near the bridge and the dam.

- The ghost of the young woman was seen along the river under the dam.

- A vanishing lady has been spotted along the road near the bridge.

- There are stories about a vanishing hitchhiker.

- A shadow person was seen running down the bank under the bridge.

- While standing on the bridge, one person had a vision of himself throwing a bag down into the water.

Investigation

Mary K. Schlais was found murdered on February 15, 1974.

A man driving a gold or orange compact car was seen pushing the body of Mary K. Schlais from the vehicle onto a township road about 13 miles east of Menomonie in Elk Lake.

Mary K. Schlais

Police believe Mary was hitchhiking and was picked up by someone in the Minneapolis (MN) area. She left for Chicago around 10:30 a.m. on Friday, February 15th. Her body was found three hours later in Elk Lake, which would not have left much time for a delay in her trip.

Police were called by a local neighbor who, upon driving towards his home, saw a man dumping something on the side of the road. The witness went to his home, which was several blocks away, and immediately phoned the police. When the police arrived, the man was gone. The witness was unable to provide a license plate number from the vehicle; however, he was able to give a description of the man and the vehicle. No backpack or books were found at the crime scene.

This case is considered a cold case, meaning that new leads have not come in, yet the case is still open. As of today, the murderer has not been arrested. There are several details that cannot be released to the public due to the status of this case.

57

We interviewed two men who recounted an experience they had one day while sitting by the dam. One turned around to look behind him, then turned back toward the water before saying to his friend, "There's a glowing, white woman behind us." His friend responded, "I know, but I'm not turning around."

According to Dunn County Sheriff John Kaanta, Mary was found nearly half a mile from the bridge. She had been repeatedly stabbed, although police determined she had not been sexually assaulted.

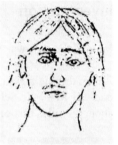

It should be noted that Sheriff Kaanta does not believe the place is haunted and had not heard reports of it being haunted until we contacted him in 1999. However, many residents in the area had heard reports of the bridge being haunted.

Suspect

Virginia Hendricks (died Feb. 1995) lived near the dam and claimed that Mary would visit her on a regular basis. Mary was described as wearing a pink angora sweater and white capri pants. She was pretty, in her early 20s, had shoulder-length blond hair, and identified herself simply as "Mary." It was believed that Mary was an apparition because she would appear at the same time every morning and afternoon, walking through Virginia's garden and tapping on her window. Virginia would bring food out to her. Mary always wore the same clothes, always showed up at the same time each day, and nobody but Virginia could see her. This happened during the Fall of 1994.

Note: *The original bridge has been demolished.*

Devil's Punch Bowl

Location: Menomonie, Dunn County, Wisconsin

Directions: From Cty Rd 25 in Menomonie, go west on Cty Rd 29 (11th Ave W which becomes Hudson Rd), turn left on Paradise Valley Rd, turn left on 410th St. The Devil's Punch Bowl will be on the left.

Ghost Lore

The Devil's Punch Bowl is considered to be both enchanted and haunted. Supposedly water collected from here will mysteriously retain its clarity and cold temperature. Gnomes have reportedly been sighted. Others have seen strange orbs of light.

Investigation

We spoke with one witness who claimed to have seen a gnome running up the side of the rock bank then bolting through the tunnel at the top.

Multiple witnesses have reported seeing a glowing orb of light, in the parking lot, that entered and passed through their automobile.

One person reported that water collected from here will retain its clarity, for up to five years and longer. One would expect it to be cloudy, considering the fact that the water contains anaerobic and aerobic bacteria and flows over fungi, moss, and bacteria growth.

She also reported that when the water is collected during a certain time of the year, it will retain its ice-cold temperature. On one occasion she collected a sample and left it in a clear bottle in the backseat of her car on a day when the temperature was in the mid-90s. Eight hours later the water was still ice cold.

History

The Devil's Punch Bowl is formed out of the Eau Claire Sandstone Formation and is part of a sea deposit that was laid down about 500 million years ago. Then it was gouged out by the glaciers about 10,000 years ago. Some fossils have been found in the rocks.

It used to be known as Black's Ravine, and it was owned by Civil War Captain Samuel Black. Later it was owned by Peter Stoll who donated it to Menomonie, and they subsequently donated it to Dunn County. Currently it is owned by the Wisconsin Farmland Conservancy of Menomonie.

The origin of the name is uncertain, but it may have been named after the UW-Stout mascot, the Blue Devil, or it may have been named after the Devil's Tower in Wyoming.

Mabel Tainter Theater

Location: Menomonie, Dunn County, Wisconsin
Proper Name: Mabel Tainter Memorial Theater
Address: 205 Main St. E., Menomonie, WI 54751-2542
Tickets: (715) 235-0001
Office: (715) 235-9726
Fax: (715) 235-9736
Email: mtainter@mabeltainter.com
Website: www.mabeltainter.com

Ghost Lore

Thought to be haunted by the ghost of Mabel Tainter.

Investigation

The staff doubt that it is the ghost of Mabel who is haunting the theatre, since she had never set foot in the building. The theatre was built after her death.

One staff member was working at the theatre during the evening when he saw a ghost of a woman dressed in white pass by him on the second floor of the theatre. The employee quit the next day.

After preparing the sound board for a show, the sound board engineer often found that when he returned in the morning, the board's settings would have been changed.

Several theatre attendees have reported seeing a ghost of a woman who often appears in the downstairs, women's bathroom. The woman is said to be curiously looking into the bathroom mirror. This woman has also been seen "walking" into and out of the bathroom.

- Several staff have seen a strange light hovering in the room used as a library and supply room. The light disappears as soon as staff get close.

- Residents of Menomonie report seeing people moving around in the building after hours when no one is present.

- Several times the security alarms have been tripped off. However, when authorities show up nothing is out of the ordinary.

- Many employees get a sense that they are not alone while spending time in the former study of Reverend Henry Doty Maxson.

- Touring actors will report seeing apparitions and strange lights while performing at the theatre.

History

Mabel Tainter, who died in 1886 at the age of nineteen, was a lover of the arts. This prompted her parents, Captain Andrew and Bertha

Tainter, to commission the construction of the theatre in 1889 as a tribute to their daughter. Captain Tainter was a wealthy lumber baron for Knapp, Stout & Company.

The Memorial was constructed during the grand Victorian era, and Andrew spared no expense in its design. The exterior of the building is constructed of Dunnville sandstone that was quarried along the Red Cedar River southeast of the present village of Downsville. The architect, Harvey Ellis, designed the Moorish style of curved surfaces, combination of arches, and hand-carved details framing the main entrance.

The lavish 313 seat theatre also served as the home to the Unitarian Society of Menomonie with Reverend Henry Doty Maxson serving as their first minister in the Mabel Tainter. The Unitarians continue to call the Mabel Tainter home.

The interior of the theatre is decorated with hand stenciled walls and ceilings, a marble staircase and floors, leaded stained-glass windows, walnut and oak woodwork, brass fixtures, and four fireplaces, each built with a different stone or technique, and a rare working Steere and Turner tracker pipe organ complete with 1,597 pipes.

The Theatre, still used as a performing arts theatre, public reading room, and cultural center, is listed on the National Register of Historic Places, is a charter member of the League of Historic American Theatres, and is a designated Wisconsin Historical Marker Site.

COULEE
REGION
WISCONSIN

Saint Charles Cemetery

Location: Cassville, Grant County, Wisconsin

Directions: From Great River Rd (Cty Rd 133) in Cassville, go east on E Crawford St, turn right on E Bluff St, turn left on Pennsylvania St which becomes St Charles Rd. Follow this through the new cemetery all the way back to the old cemetery.

Ghost Lore

People have reported seeing balls of light late at night in the old section of the cemetery.

Investigation

We found a little dirt road that leads from the new cemetery back to the old cemetery, which is isolated and concealed by the woods, resting upon a hillside.

There are power lines that pass overhead through the graveyard. According to some scientists, ball lightning can apparently travel along such wires. Whether this is a possible explanation remains to be seen. Further investigation is necessary.

The Subway Ghost

Location: Dodgeville, Iowa County, Wisconsin
Address: 1400 State Road 23, Dodgeville, WI 53533-2111
Phone: (608) 935-5889

Ghost Lore

Items will fly off the shelves or fall to the floor on their own. An extremely foul stench will permeate the building. The beepers on the doors will constantly go off for no reason. Employees reported that they have heard their names being called, but could not find the source.

A couple of employees have reported seeing an apparition of a woman who is skinny, about 50 years old, and wearing a dress, who stands by the cash register and gives them dirty looks. Whenever they attempt to approach her, she disappears.

The Dare: If you go into the basement after 9:00 p.m., things will fly off the shelves onto the floor.

Note: *Only employees are allowed in the basement.*

Investigation

The Subway Restaurant is located on the site that was formerly a Harley Davidson shop owned by Al Forbes from Cobb, Wisconsin. He had inherited the real estate and business from his parents, Mr. & Mrs. Eugene Forbes, also of Cobb, who were both tragically killed in a head-on collision in the early 1980s. The accident occurred at the creek bridge south of Arthur, Wisconsin on Hwy. 80. A carload of teenagers driving over 100 mph crossed the center line and struck them head-on killing the passengers in both vehicles. It is believed by some that the apparition of the woman seen in Subway is Mrs. Forbes.

The store has had strange things happen since about 2000. The three employees we spoke with informed us that the haunting is not confined to the basement. They reported that large stacks of cups would suddenly fall over, and employees would walk to get something and the sandwiches that they did not cut would be cut. Many of the employees believed that the place was haunted, and it was well known among the work staff. We did not notice any paranormal activity during our investigation.

Whiskers Olde Tyme Inn

Location: Genoa, Vernon County, Wisconsin
Correction: Several sources erroneously refer to it as Big River Restaurant
Address: 500 Main St., Genoa, WI 54632
Phone: (608) 689-2652

Ghost Lore

The previous owner was named "Kenny." He used to watch only CNN, and he would drink eight cups of coffee a day. He died, and his ghost haunts the restaurant.

- When the current owner shuts off the lights and locks up at night, often the lights will turn back on.

- People have heard footsteps on the basement stairs.

- Eight coffee cups (the number Kenny drank per day) are missing.

- Dishes have mysteriously disappeared.

- When employees leave the room and return, they find the TV has changed channels to CNN.

Investigation

Kenneth Beck was the previous owner. He did watch CNN and kept the TV exclusively on that channel. We were, however, unable to verify that he drank precisely eight cups of coffee per day. He had a heart attack and died outside the building near the dumpster. Kenny died in either October or November of 1999 and was about 60 years old at the time of his death. Right after he died the furnace quit working, and the haunting activity began.

"Arden," another former owner, used to live upstairs. He collapsed and later died.

Many years ago there was a roller skating rink in the upstairs of the building. At one time there was a terrible accident on the Mississippi River, and the rink was used as a makeshift morgue.

The current owner, Patty Ziegler, reports that the lights, stereo, and television will mysteriously turn on by themselves. Often she will lock up for the night, only to return in the morning and find the TV, stereo, lights, grill, and coffee maker turned on. She confirms that mysterious footsteps have been heard on the basement steps when nobody was there.

Neither the current owner nor any of the employees had ever heard of eight coffee cups being missing.

The owner stated that half their dinner plates and several glasses had disappeared. Neither the owner nor any of the employees were regular viewers of CNN. They usually kept the TV tuned to ESPN,

71

but confirmed that the TV would frequently switch channels to CNN by itself. Mary Jo, one of the employees, would become visibly upset each time it happened.

Patty also owns The Big River Inn, located directly behind Whiskers. Employees report that rooms B4 and B3 are haunted. The doors to these rooms will mysteriously close by themselves. We did inspect the rooms and found that the doors were not level and that gravity would cause them to close on their own.

The Bodega Brew Pub

Location: La Crosse, La Crosse County, Wisconsin
AKA: Pearl Street Brewery
Address: 122 4th St. S., La Crosse, WI 54601-3201
Phone: (608) 782-0677
Hours: Daily noon - 2:30 am
Payment Methods: Cash, VISA, MasterCard

Ghost Lore

The Bodega Brew Pub is said to be haunted by a former owner who refuses to leave the property. Many staff have reported getting strange feelings while going down into the basement. Staff have reported hearing ghostly voices while working at the bar.

History

The Bodega Brew Pub was once known as the Union Saloon. Paul Malin owned the property when it was a pool hall, and ran it until his death in 1901. After Malin's death the property changed hands several times. A startling confession came from owner A.J. Himes when he reported that he was selling the property because of the ghosts that haunted the place. The pub has changed hands several times throughout the years, but the ghost stays the same.

Investigation

We spoke with several employees who have had personal experiences.

- One employee moved some bricks into a pile against a door in the basement and went back upstairs. A few minutes later he returned to the basement to find that the bricks were un-piled and put back in their original position.

- Often staff and customers will hear the sounds of a woman in high heels walking down in the basement when no one is down there.

- One employee reported that he saw an apparition of a man while cleaning up after the bar had closed. The ghost was walking through the bar and did not seem to notice the employee.

Most of the ghost stories started to surface after the death of Paul Malin, and many believe he still resides at the old pub.

Del's Bar

Location: La Crosse, La Crosse County, Wisconsin
Address: 229 3rd St. N., La Crosse, WI 54601-3208
Phone: (608) 784-4990
Hours: Mon-Thu 2 pm-2 am, Fri-Sun 11 am-2:30 am
Payment Methods: Cash only

Ghost Lore

This unassuming neighborhood bar has been in operation since the 1930s. The inside of the bar represents a wide range of tastes from Green Bay Packers gear to cast metal cars. However, the most interesting thing in the bar is the ghost. Several workers and customers believe that the bar is haunted by several ghosts.

Investigation

- We spoke with several employees that informed us of several strange happenings at Dels's. A bartender named Luke would often report seeing an apparition of a man when he ventured downstairs. Many of the reports of ghosts and eerie noises come from the basement.

- Other employees report hearing strange noises while they are alone in the bar. Another bartender has heard many voices and strange sounds over the last seven years he has been at Del's. These sounds range from hearing voices calling their name to sounds of people talking when no one is present.

- Customers will report seeing what appears to be a ghost out of the corner of their eye. However, when they turn to directly look at the ghost, it vanishes.

The Mineral Point Vampire

Location: Graceland Cemetery, Mineral Point, Iowa
County, Wisconsin

Directions: From US 151 in Mineral Point, go west on
Fair St. The cemetery is on the left.

Ghost Lore

A Mineral Point police officer was reported to have seen and
given chase to a vampire that was rummaging around the cemetery. The vampire was said to have scaled a tall fence, with
supernatural abilities, to escape from the officer.

Investigation

- In April of 1981, Mineral Point police officer John Pepper was on evening patrol when he passed by Graceland Cemetery. Mr. Pepper noticed what he said was a very tall, extremely pale, thin, Dracula-looking vampire wearing a black trench coat. Mr. Pepper gave chase to the vampire, only to witness it easily hurdle a large fence. It was then that Mr. Pepper lost sight of the vampire. Police did search for the vampire, believing it was an April Fools' joke, yet they were unable to find it.

- The case received international attention and put intense pressure on John Pepper. Shortly after the encounter, John Pepper moved away from Mineral Point.

- We were unable to contact Mr. Pepper; however, we did speak with several residents of Mineral Point who informed us that they thought of Mr. Pepper as a practical joker. They told the story that John and a friend would often dress up as an ape and run around town. We also cannot rule out the theory that Mr. Pepper was an unknowing participant in a hoax for April Fools Day.

The Walker House

Location: Mineral Point, Iowa County, Wisconsin
Address: 1 Water St., Mineral Point, WI 53565-1359

Ghost Lore

This historic inn is said to be the home of many permanent guests, most notably, the ghost of William Caffee, who was hanged right next to the property.   It is also rumored that in the early 1880s, a man stole a horse from a farmer and went for a drink at the Walker House.   While he was enjoying his drink, a mob found him and hanged him outside the Walker House.

History

The Walker House was constructed by Irishman William Walker in 1836 and was an immediate success. Many refer to the house as the Mineral Point Hotel.

On November 1, 1842, William Caffee was hanged in public for killing Samuel Southwick while in a heated argument. Over 5,000 people came out to witness the first public hanging. Mr. Caffee was said to have been brought to the gallows alongside his coffin, beating out a tune of a funeral march with empty beer bottles. This defiance for authority seemed to carry over into his death.

After Walker died in 1900, Charles Curtis purchased the building. Curtis did little work on the Walker house before he passed away in 1930. In 1950, the property was sold to Ben Bollerude. Mr. Bollerude rented rooms at the Walker for five years before the state closed the home.

In 1957, the inn closed down and was vacant for several years. Unfortunately the abandoned building become run-down and was victim to vandalism.

In 1964, the inn was purchased by Ted Landon. Mr. Landon had a grand vision of restoring the inn to its original glory.

In 1974, Landon reopened the inn for business. However, business was slow, and after only four years, Landon and his partners sold the inn to Dr. David Ruf.

Investigation

Jack Holzhueter, of the State Historical Society, has cast doubt on the origins of this case. In his 1979 article, "Then and Now," Holzhueter questions whether there even was a Walker House in 1842. He believes that the land was not even purchased from the government until 1845. His research would mean that Caffeee was killed long before a hotel was on the land.

There is also some doubt cast on the story of how Caffee was brought to the gallows. According to Janice Terrill, the November 4, 1842 newspaper article did not mention any story of Caffee having beer bottles. She too speculated that the Walker did not exist in 1836 as claimed. She also believes that many of the ghost stories are a recent phenomenon.

Regardless of the real history, many workers and owners have had an experience at the Walker House. During restoration, Mr. Landon started to experience strange incidents, including hearing heavy breathing and mysterious footsteps.

Dr. Ruf reported many of the same unexplained activities as Landon. Ruf also experienced strange voices whose origins were never located. An apparition of a headless man was spotted in the dining room during 1981.

Former worker Walker Calvert states he had daily contact with two ghosts from 1978 through 1982. Calvert, the manager and chef at the restaurant, often heard strange noises and had mysterious pranks played on him by the ghost of Caffee. Among the ghosts Calvert saw was an old man in tattered clothing. This encounter was unique in that it lasted for several minutes. The witness reported that the ghost was wearing an old, grey suit reminiscent of the

mining era.   Calvert also claims to have spoken with the ghost on numerous occasions.

Former worker Katie Dyke stated that on one occasion she and Calvert witnessed a bread box move on its own.

Staff reports that the ghost often locked doors, pulled hair, and snuck up on people. Another owner has also had experiences at the Walker House. Harvey Glanzer reports that twice in 1985, he left for home and the door was in place, and when he returned home the door was placed to the side.

It is reported that in 1984, an exorcism was performed that got rid of seven spirits that were said to haunt the place. Regardless of the exorcism, many visitors still claim that the ghost of William Caffee remains in the house he loved.

Ghost Dancer

Location: Osseo, Trempealeau County, Sumner Township, Wisconsin

Directions: From Osseo, take Hwy 53 two miles south to the junction of Cty Rd H.

Ghost Lore

About 20 years ago, an 18-year-old Native American resident of Osseo died in a tragic car accident when his car plunged into a pond, and he drowned. By some accounts, his body was found in the back seat of the car; by other accounts, his shoelaces were tangled around the gas petal.

There have been reports of daytime apparitions of an Indian wearing traditional Native American regalia appearing at the scene of the accident, dancing and performing ritual, who later vanishes.

83

Investigation

A nineteen-year-old Native American John Thunder drowned in his late-model Oldsmobile at about 12:30 a.m. on May 21, 1984 when he failed to stop at the stop sign at Hwy 53. His auto struck the embankment and slid into a 12-foot-deep irrigation pond near the highway.

He was a resident of Osseo and had worked as a clerk in a retail store. Mr. Thunder was buried in the Fairchild Cemetery in Fairchild, Wisconsin.

The Ghost Dancer was first spotted in 1989 and then again in 1996. These sightings did not actually occur at the location where he died; they were seen near a scenic overlook that is considered a sacred site.

FOX
VALLEY
WISCONSIN

Appleton Curling Club

Location: Appleton, Outagamie County, Wisconsin
Address: 615 E. North St., Appleton, WI 54911-5557
Phone: (920) 954-8987
Website: www.appletoncurlingclub.com
Membership: Single membership is $270 for the season;
Family membership is $385. These fees include unlimited ice
time and access to the club. First time curlers receive a 50%
discount for the first year.

Ghost Lore

The building is said to be haunted by former members of the club
who continue to visit the club after their death. Apparitions are said
to be seen in the viewers box. Strange smells have been reported
throughout the club.

History

The Appleton Curling Club was established in 1939. Ray Fallon and Harold Mather each owned some curling equipment and decided to purchase addition "stones" from the High Park Club to create their own park. Two sheets of ice were created out of the Pierce Park tennis courts. However, due to weather difficulties, including snow, frequent thaws, and a lack of lighting, the site was short lived.

In 1940, the pair rented a concrete chicken house on Highway OO. Water was provided to the site through a rural well. This process proved difficult as the water had to be force fed through over 100 feet of pipe to the chicken house, where it was then carried alongside the building and placed in barrels. These barrels were ultimately dumped onto the surface until a satisfactory level of ice was created.

After three years the club was unable to continue when their bid on the rented land was beaten by a chicken farmer. It was during this winter that members decided to construct their own curling

building. The building was set to be built in Pierce Park.

Even with war gobbling up materials, the building was ready for use for the 1944-45 season and completely finished for the 1945-46 season. The 1st annual Men's Invitational Bonspiel competition was held in January of 1946.

In 1951, the club started installing pipes to provide refrigeration, along with completing the addition of 1952. The popularity of the club forced the group to find a larger facility, and in January of 1960, the club moved to its current location.

Disaster struck the club in 1967 when fire ripped through the club-house and upstairs spectator-viewing box. These areas were rebuilt and are still used by many curlers and fans today.

Investigation

We spoke with several members of the club including one of the icemakers.

Many reports came from the bar/lounge area where several bartenders report drastic temperature changes both cold and warm.

A former member of the club named Ken had a physical disability that resulted in a distinct walk. After his death, many workers have reported hearing Ken's "walk" on the second floor while no one else was in the building. Oftentimes, the walking noise is so apparent that workers will speak to Ken.

An icemaker reported that several times while he had been working alone in the club, he looked up to the viewing box to discover a ghost staring down at him. The ghost had its hands in its face watching as though it was checking up on the icemakers' work. The icemakers believed that the ghost was a former member of the club.

One former member named Ed was known for smoking his tobacco pipe. Shortly after his death, many workers started reporting that while they were alone, they became surrounded by a strange tobacco scent of unknown origin. Several icemakers have also reported the distinct tobacco scent while simultaneously getting the feeling they were being watched by some unseen presence.

Late night cleaners report seeing ghostly apparitions pass by them while they are cleaning the viewing room. These sighting were enough to convince one woman to never visit the viewing room alone. Cleaners also have seen and heard the doors leading to and from the viewing room slam shut on their own accord.

Hearthstone Mansion

Location: Appleton, Outagamie County, Wisconsin
Official Name: Hearthstone Historic House Museum
AKA: Hearthstone Museum
Address: 625 W. Prospect Ave., Appleton, WI 54911-6042
Phone: (920) 730-8204
Website: www.focol.org/hearthstone
Email: hearthstonemuseum@athenet.net
Hours: Open Memorial Day to Labor Day: Tue-Fri, 10 am to 4 pm, Sat 1 to 4 pm; Labor Day to Memorial Day: Tue and Thu 10 am to 4 pm. Closed Sundays.

Ghost Lore

This Victorian home is believed to be haunted by one of its former owners, entrepreneur and philanthropist A. W. Priest.

Investigation

A. W. Priest (1848-1930) was the second owner of this elegant home, and it is believed that he died in the house. Reportedly, each morning when the office manager unlocks the front doors, she offers a polite salutation of "Good morning, Mr. Priest" to the unseen spirit. Others have reported hearing strange sounds, including the distinct sound of somebody sneezing, when nobody else was in the building. Volunteers working in the museum have frequently reported the uneasy feeling of Mr. Priest's presence.

History

On September 30, 1882, this historic home became the first residence in the world to be lighted from a centrally located hydroelectric plant. Henry J. Rogers, a prominent Appleton industrialist, built and lighted this house using the same power source that lighted his paper mill. The original Edison light fixtures are still used in the house.

In 1900, A. W. Priest bought the house and lived there until his death in 1930. In 1931, John Badenoch rented the house and used it as a restaurant known as the Hearthstone. Eventually it was turned into a museum.

Kate Blood

Location: Riverside Cemetery, Appleton, Outagamie County, Wisconsin
Address: 714 N. Owaissa St., Appleton, WI 54911-5226
Phone: (920) 733-5629

Directions: In the Riverside Cemetery, drive to Block D, follow the chained off path that goes down the hill towards the river. Kate Blood's grave will be on the left.

Ghost Lore

Kate Blood murdered her husband and three children then took her own life.

The gravestones of her husband and three kids are located in a small remote region of the graveyard cut off from the rest of the cemetery to hide her gruesome crime.

If you visit Kate's gravestone at midnight on a full moon night, you will see a substance that looks like blood oozing out from the top, right corner of her stone; however, this liquid is dry to the touch.

Investigation

- We found no evidence of Kate Blood ever having children with her husband George M. Miller.

- We found that Kate Blood did not kill her husband George, as he went on to wed Mary Moulton Hutchinson after Kate had passed away.

- We spoke with several witnesses who claimed to have seen the "blood" oozing out of the tombstone; unfortunately, we did not witness this ourselves.

- Several local residents reported to us that they saw apparitions and shadowy figures near Kate's gravesite and throughout Riverside Cemetery.

- The cemetery groundskeeper had not heard of Kate's story, yet she had heard rumors of the cemetery being haunted.

- The three gravestones around Kate's marker do not represent her three children, they contain Kate M. Blood; her husband, George Miller; and George's second wife.

Zuelke Building

Location: Appleton, Outagamie County, Wisconsin
Address: 103 W. College Ave., Appleton, WI 54911-5770

Ghost Lore

Whenever anything goes wrong at the Zuelke Building, people there blame it on the ghost of Irving Zuelke who is rumored to haunt the building.

Investigation

The cleaning crew frequently reports ghostly activity while working late at night. One worker reported that in 1996 he was sweeping a stairwell when he felt someone tap him on the shoulder.   He turned around and saw half a body and a hand disappear into the wall.

During a reception in 1990, a pianist was hired to play on the second floor balcony. When the musician took a break, all the elevators in the building simultaneously stopped working. As soon as the pianist resumed playing the piano, the elevators mysteriously began to move again. It was well known that Irving Zuelke was a pianist and music lover, and many people believe his spirit was active there that day.

History

The 12-story Zuelke Building opened in 1932. Standing at 168 feet, it was the tallest building in Appleton until 1952.

Corner of Breed and State

Location: Chilton, Chilton Township, Calumet County, Wisconsin
Official Names: West Breed Street and North State Street

Directions: From US 151 go north on N Main St for less than a mile, arrive at the intersection of N State St and W Breed St (Cty Rd F).

Ghost Lore

Witnesses report seeing a feeble, pale, old woman wearing a royal blue scarf and a blue jacket who vanishes before their eyes.

Investigation

According to a resident who lives on one of the corners of the inter-section, there was an old woman, who lived across the street from him, who died a couple of years ago. However, he has neither witnessed an apparition nor does he know of anyone who has.

We do have an eyewitness account from somebody who drove through this intersection with a carload of friends when they spotted a large orb of light hovering in the air that changed position and began to follow their vehicle. One of the passengers entered into an altered state of consciousness. She was incoherent and began to behave abnormally and to utter strange things. After about 10 minutes, she snapped out of it, and had no recollection of the incident.

The Dare: It is said that in this same area is a street where if you drag race with another car, a phantom hearse will appear and race with your vehicle.

Note: *The authors do not advocate street racing.*

Lawrence Cemetery

Location: De Pere, Brown County, Wisconsin
AKA: Cady Cemetery or Old Cady Cemetery
Corrections: Some sources erroneously refer to it as St. Lawrence Cemetery

Directions: From Cty Rd EE in De Pere, go south on Sand Acres Drive. The cemetery is on the right.

Ghost Lore

People have reported a variety of strange happenings in this cemetery. They have heard strange sounds, including growling. Mysterious fog has been encountered, that is seen only in the cemetery and not in the surrounding terrain. Some have witnessed the scary orbs of light that are so often reported in cemeteries, and they have seen other unexplained lights late at night. One of the most commonly reported experiences is the uncontrollable feeling of trepidation that overtakes people.

Investigation

We have a first-hand account of three people who visited the cemetery at 6:00 p.m. one evening. They noticed a light in the window of the cemetery storage shed. The light was on for about 90 seconds, went off for about 5 minutes, was on again for about 30 seconds, then went off and remained off. There was no groundskeeper there at the time.

As they departed from the cemetery, the three visitors reported that they sensed a strange negative energy or presence and had the feeling of not being welcome. They felt that they were being spiritually attacked, and reported feeling "numbness, partial convulsion symptoms, tension, butterflies in the stomach, weakness, internal organs hurting, migraine headaches, pain in the neck, partial paralysis of the left side of the body, and slight nausea" that lasted for about one to two hours.

Octagon House

Location: Fond du Lac, Fond du Lac County, Wisconsin
Official Name: The Historic 1856 Octagon House
Address: 276 Linden S., Fond du Lac, WI 54935-495
Phone: (920) 922-1608 or (920) 923-5656
National Register of Historic Places #72000051

Ghost Lore

Apparitions of a young boy who roams the house.

Investigation

We spoke with the owner. He never witnessed any apparitions, but verified that strange things regularly happen in the house. On one occasion, he stepped out of a room for a moment and returned only to find the spinning wheel to be completely disassembled. It is common to find objects to be moved or misplaced.

History

This restored, 12-room home was originally built in 1856 as an Indian fort, and holds a rich history. Once used as a part of the Underground Railroad, this house contains nine passageways, a secret room, and a hand-dug underground tunnel.

The house was featured on the History Channel's *Hidden Passages* program.

Downtown YMCA

Location: Green Bay, Brown County, Wisconsin
Address: 235 N. Jefferson St., Green Bay, WI 54301-5126
Phone: (920) 436-9622

Ghost Lore

This historic, five-story, brick building squarely centered in the business district of Green Bay is reported to be haunted by a man in his early 20s who was said to be murdered on the property. It is rumored that the YMCA is home to many eerie reports of a ghost lurking around the second floor while YMCA members are busy in training. Other staff are reported to have witnessed the ghost of the young man while doing routine cleaning. The ghost has been described as a young man in his 20s with an appearance that indicates he may have died long ago. The ghost apparently does not notice the other members of the YMCA and reportedly goes about his usual business.

Investigation

- The Berners-Schober & Associates designed building was con-structed in 1925, and was built as a YMCA.

- Throughout the years, the building has undergone several minor renovations, including the installation of a swimming pool in 1967.

- Even with several renovations, the YMCA still possesses its original walls.

- The building houses five floors and an attic; however, floors four and five and the attic are used for storage.

- Prior to 1980, the YMCA housed residents on those floors, a practice that later ended. According to historians, it was during that time that three deaths occurred, although we were unable to get specific dates. The first death took place as a resident accidentally started a fire on his hot plate and had to evacuate the facility. While he was leaving, he discovered that he had left his wallet in the room and went back into the building for it. It was on this return trip that he died of smoke inhalation. The second death is attributed to a man that was stabbed to death in the hallway. And the third known death was a man that was shot to death in the TV room while he was watching television.

- We spoke with several staff who have never had a personal experience, yet many exchange stories passed on by members fortunate enough to witness the young man.

- If the ghost is that of one of those who passed away on the premises, we are unsure which one it may be.

Dartford Cemetery

Location: Green Lake, Green Lake County, Wisconsin

Directions: From Hwy 23, go east on North St. The cemetery will be on both the north and south sides of the street. The mausoleum is located on the south side.

Ghost Lore

Situated in a quiet part of the town of Green Lake is a cemetery where restless spirits supposedly rise up at night. People report seeing dark figures hiding in the shadows and orbs of light darting between gravestones. Some visitors to the cemetery notice strange sounds. Others experience the eerie sensation of being followed or watched.

Sometimes the apparitions are vivid enough to be recognized as Civil War soldiers, perhaps wandering through the graveyard in search of fallen comrades.

On more than one occasion, the ghost of an Indian chief has been seen. It is a chief from a local tribe who originally lived in the area and drowned after he had too much "firewater" to drink and was attempting to swim across the Fox River on a dare.

It is believed that a mausoleum in the cemetery contains the bodies of several children from the same family who all died from polio.

The Dare: If you sit on the roof of the mausoleum, the ghost of one of the children will violently shove you off.

Investigation

The Ho-Chunk nation inhabited this area in the 1600s when Father Marquette first ventured into the area. The tribe lived peacefully with the white settlers that later arrived. In 1832, the Ho-Chunk signed a treaty that ceded all territory east and south of the Fox and Wisconsin Rivers. Most of the Ho-Chunk ended up on reservations. The last chief to rule the Green Lake Area was Chief

Highknocker. His Indian name was Hanageh, but the white settlers referred to him as Highknocker because of the stovepipe hat that he always wore.

The Ho-Chunk considered the shores of Green Lake to be sacred because it was believed to be the home of the Water Spirit. It was expected that each member of the tribe make at least one pilgrimage to the lake for their traditional ceremonies. Some, such as Chief Highknocker, returned every summer. In the summer of 1911, he was returning home, but found that there was no canoe available to get across the river, so he attempted to swim across and accidentally drowned. He was buried along the bank of the river, so it is curious that people would report seeing his apparition in the Dartford cemetery.

Note: *We do not encourage people to sit or stand on the roof of the mausoleum.*

Hilbert Road

Location: Hilbert, Calumet County, Wisconsin

Directions: From Hwy 32/57 in Hilbert go east on W Main St, turn right on N 1st St. The road will turn left and become E Main St. Follow it until it becomes Hilbert Rd. Eventually Hilbert Rd turns right. Follow it until you see the lone tree on the side of the road.

Ghost Lore

A young girl was killed on Hilbert Road, just outside the town of Hilbert, in the early 1900s. At night, the ghost of her father vigilantly waits by a lone tree and sometimes wanders the road in search of his beloved daughter.

The ghost of a man carrying a lantern and missing one side of his face has been seen wandering the road at night and stopping people to ask them if they have seen his daughter who never came home.

The Dare: If you visit the road between midnight and 5:00 a.m., the ghost will be seen standing under a lone tree on the side of the road. If you shine a light on him, he will disappear.

Investigation

It is curious that it was the daughter who died, yet it is the ghost of the father that haunts the road. Also, no explanation has been offered as to why he is missing half his face.

We did interview some of the local residents of Hilbert. Some were familiar with the haunting, but told us that the young girl had died in more recent years, not in the early 1900s.

Valley Road

Location: Menasha, Winnebago County, Wisconsin

Directions: From Hwy 10 in Menasha, take Cty Rd 47 north, turn left on Valley Rd, drive to Palisades Park area.

Ghost Lore

About 100 years ago a young groom was killed on the way to his wedding when his horse-drawn carriage was in an accident on Valley Road in Menasha, and he was thrown into a tree and strangled to death by his own bow tie.

On certain nights you can see an apparition of the groom hanging from a tree.

Investigation

This account is reminiscent of the story of Absolom in the Bible:

> And Absalom was seated on his mule, and the mule went under the thick branches of a great tree, and his head became fixed in the tree and he was lifted up between earth and heaven, and the beast under him went on (2 Samuel 18:9).

Valley Road east of Hwy. 47 is technically within the Appleton city limits, so we focused our investigation on the western stretch of the road, which is within Menasha. The only tree that overhangs the road is the one on the north side of the road directly across from Saint John's Cemetery; however, others report it as having occurred on the stretch of road between Palisades Park and the Old Town Hall at 1000 Valley Road.

The Grand Opera House

Location: Oshkosh, Winnebago County, Wisconsin
Street Address: 100 High Ave., Oshkosh, WI 54901-4809
Mailing Address: PO Box 1004, Oshkosh, WI 54903-1004
Phone Numbers:
    (920) 424-2350 (Box Office Phone)
    (866) 96GRAND (Box Office Toll-Free)
    (920) 424-2357 (Fax)
    (920) 424-2355 (Administrative Phone)
Website: www.grandoperahouse.org

Ghost Lore

This historic theatre located in Downtown Oshkosh is said to be
haunted by the spirits of former workers who continue to be
involved in productions. Visiting actors report encountering
strange apparitions throughout the theatre. Mysterious phantom
dogs are said to wander the historic theatre.

Investigation

We spoke with several staff members of the Grand Opera House and were given an opportunity to investigate the theatre.

Much of the ghost history began in 1967, when University of Wisconsin–Oshkosh Professor Bob Jacobs took his class to the Grand to film a fictional movie about a haunted theatre. While shooting the film, Professor Jacobs and his students spotted a ghost with small round glasses. The class became convinced that they had encountered the ghost of Percy Keene. The ghost was said to have been standing in the balcony looking down at them with a big smile on his face. The class apparently described Mr. Keene's haircut and small round glasses perfectly. Mr. Keene was a former stage manager of the theatre. Mr. Keene had been involved with the theatre from 1895 up until his death in 1967.

During the filming of his movie, the professor believed that the ghost of Percy Keene also saved the life of one of his students. During a scene in one of the plays, assistant Larry Schroeder was suspending high above the stage for about an hour. When he was finally brought back down, the minute his feet touched the stage floor, the rope that was holding him suddenly broke. Jacobs thought that this was extremely strange that a rope would snap without any pressure on it, and was thoroughly convinced that Keene had intervened. While watching a sneak preview of his movie in the theatre, Jacobs looked up into the balcony and saw the ghost of Percy Keene smiling down at him, as though he was showing his support to the crew.

We were told of the encounter that the executive director had as he sat in the theatre. The director would often go to the theatre and sit in the darkness to wind down and clear his mind. As he was leaving the theatre, he had an overwhelming urge to turn around and look at the stage. It was there, onstage, that he noticed a vaporous orange mist hovering about.

Many performers report that while they are rehearsing, they see

113

ghosts sitting in the theatre as though they are watching the play. The staff told us that when they check up on these stories, they find the seats have been pushed down where the ghosts were said to have been sitting.

The balcony is home to much of the paranormal phenomena reported, as we were told of the experience of a light director who reportedly saw a dog down on stage and quickly asked the actors to remove the dog from the stage. The actors, puzzled by the request, replied that there was no dog on the stage. Many other performers report chilling encounters with this phantom dog. Often phantom footsteps are heard coming up the staircase, yet to the surprise of the witness, no one ever comes up.

History

The Grand was constructed in 1883. Planning for the Grand began one year earlier in 1882 when several local business leaders expressed dissatisfaction with the state of Oshkosh's theatre. Being that Oshkosh was the second largest city in Wisconsin, the town believed that they needed a theatre suited for their stature in the state.

The Grand was constructed by Oshkosh resident William Waters. Waters was well known throughout Wisconsin for many of his other creations.

On August 9th, the Grand Theatre opened with the play "The Bohemian Girl" by the C.D. Hess Opera Company.

The theatre had an official count of 921 seats. However, many nights more chairs were brought in and often theatregoers would stand. This raised the number of people in the Grand to over 1,000.

In 1885, electric lights replaced the outdated gas jets that had been lighting the theatre. In 1891, a hotel was built across the street from the Grand to accommodate all the new visitors to Oshkosh.

The theatre continued to entertain and impress through the early 1900s. In the late 1920s the theatre was shut down in order to perform some much needed remodeling and redecorating. These improvements included an updated heating system, ventilation, lighting, and plumbing.

With the rise of motion pictures, the theatre was sold in 1948, and converted into a movie house showing second-run movies. The theatre also changed its name to the Civic Theatre.

In 1950, the theatre's name was changed back to the Grand Theatre and more remodeling took place. To the displeasure of many residents, the Athearn Hotel that was located across the street was shut down. Determined to not let the Grand suffer the same fate, Oshkosh residents vowed to keep the Grand operating at any cost.

The citizens succeeded in their mission; however, the outcome was not quite what they expected, as the Grand became an X-rated movie house. In 1974, the Grand was possibly the only X-rated theatre to be placed on the Register of Historic Places.

In 1980, residents voted overwhelmingly to restore and engage in the operation of the Grand Opera House. The city of Oshkosh stepped forward and bought the building. Much of the theatre was remodeled and renovated. On October of 1982, the Grand Theatre Restoration Project was underway.

On September 27, 1986, the Grand had its reopening dedication and on October 3rd, the Grand had another grand opening. To pay homage to the 100-year history, the Grand opened with "The Bohemian Girl," the very first play ever to run at the grand.

In 1989, the Oshkosh Opera House Foundation was granted permission to use the theatre as a presenting/rental hall. In November of the same year, the Oshkosh Opera House Foundation was granted a lease of the building from the city.

The Grand Opera House continues to entertain and delight audiences to this day.

New Moon Café

Location: Oshkosh, Winnebago County, Wisconsin
Address: 401 N. Main St., Oshkosh, WI 54901-4907
Phone: (920) 232-0976
Website: www.newmooncafe.com
Email: info@newmooncafe.com

Ghost Lore

It is rumored that this unique coffee house is haunted by several ghosts who passed away in the Great Oshkosh Fire. Staff tell the story of encountering an apparition of a young man while going downstairs. The young man is described as wearing what appears to be a bellboy uniform. Customers report seeing the ghost of an elderly woman that appears in the main lobby. It is believed that this woman also died in the Great Oshkosh Fire. When she is seen by staff and customers, she is always well dressed and has a sophisticated look about her. Mysterious voices and noises have been reported by both staff and customers.

Investigation

- The original building, the Beckwith, was destroyed by the Great Oshkosh Fire of 1875, but it is widely believed that nobody died in the building.

- A woman did die in the building. However, it was not during the Great Oshkosh Fire. Mrs. Simon Paige died during the fire of 1880. Mrs. Paige was the wife of a wealthy retired lumberman. It is extremely likely that Mrs. Paige would have dressed in a manner consistent with her lifestyle and wealth.

- We found no evidence of a bellhop dying on the property.

- We spoke with several eyewitnesses who had a personal experience with the ghost of the young man, and they did describe him as looking like a bellhop.

- Several of the staff told stories of getting eerie sensations while downstairs and a few even encountered the ghost of Mrs. Paige.

History

1854 – Shingles manufacturer Sanford Beckwith moves to town from Oneida County, New York.

1867 – The Empire House building is constructed by James A. Rea.

1873 – The building becomes a pharmacy and is run by George and John Bauman.

1873 – Mr. Rea sells the building to Sanford Beckwith who then renames it the Beckwith House.

1875 – The Great Oshkosh Fire destroys the building.

1876 – With the help of S.A. Fargo, Beckwith builds a new version of the hotel.

1878 – Beckwith is elected mayor of Oshkosh.

1880 – The Beckwith building is a success with all floors occupied.

1880 – Another fire destroys the building killing one woman and damaging over $50,000 of the building. The house is rebuilt, yet this time it is only two stories. The hotel is no longer operating.

1916 – The drug store still operates in the building.

1920s – Businesses are moving in and out of the building.

1929 – Bauman sells his family's pharmacy business to Walgreens.

1934 – Walgreens is the sole occupant of the building

1954 – Walgreens goes out of business and the property remains vacant.

1957 – The House of Cards and Camera moves into the building.

1970s-1980s – Several different businesses move in and out of the building.

1990s – The same pattern of businesses moving in and out continues.

Currently – The building is home to New Moon Café.

Riverside Cemetery

Location: Oshkosh, Winnebago County, Wisconsin
Address: 1901 Algoma Blvd., Oshkosh, WI 54901-2103
Phone: (920) 236-5092

Ghost Lore

Apparitions of children frolic in the cemetery at night.

Investigation

An eyewitness claims to have seen a small child of about five years old with curly blonde locks, wearing a beautiful, frilly party dress, but without shoes and a coat. She was quite a distance away, but she looked directly at him and waved. His first response was to look around for the child's parents because she was not dressed warm enough for the cold weather. There was absolutely no one else in the cemetery. When he turned back to look at the little girl,

119

she was gone. He looked around the headstones for a few minutes but could not find her. About three days later, she appeared to him in a dream and revealed that her name was "Clara."

We visited the cemetery with a psychic who was unaware of the history of the cemetery, yet she sensed the presence and movement of the ghosts of children.

Starseed

Location: Oshkosh, Winnebago County, Wisconsin
Address: 457 N. Main St., Oshkosh, WI 54901-4907
Phone: (920) 303-9230

Ghost Lore

Star Seed is a new age store that deals with spirituality, spirits, and new age philosophy and gifts. Located directly off Main Street in downtown Oshkosh, Starseed is part of the Historic Beckwith Block, named after former owner of the property, Sanford Beckwith. It is said that customers will report seeing a phantom cat running around the upstairs of the building. Many young children will also report playing with a mysterious young child. Numerous customers have left the building with a sense that they did indeed experience a ghost while shopping at Starseed. The staff have encountered several apparitions while spending time in the building.

Investigation

• We spoke with Starseed's owners and staff who informed us that they believe that the store is indeed haunted by several ghosts. One of those ghosts is that of a young child who died an accidental death while playing upstairs. The owners believe the child was playing with a ball when the ball rolled down the stairs. The child excitedly went after the ball, tumbled down the stairs, and died due to injuries suffered during the fall.

• The owners chose to keep the name of the child who passed away a secret. Apparently, a few years ago, a psychic came in to investigate the store and gained a sense that a young child had passed away in the building. The psychic also sensed several other spirits in the building.

• We were unable to locate the death record of any child passing away in the store.

• Staff report hearing footsteps originating from the second floor. However, when the staff go to investigate, they find that no one else is in the building. Staff also tell stories of strange behavior with the lighting, as many times lights that were turned off will be found turned back on and visa versa.

• Many staff have witnessed a phantom cat that is usually spotted near the second floor steps where the accidental death of the child is said to have taken place. Other customers have seen the cat racing around upstairs. This phantom cat has also been known to disappear right into thin air.

Readfield Graveyard

Location: Readfield, Waupaca County, Wisconsin
Proper Name: Evangelical Lutheran Zions Cemetery

Directions: From Hwy 10 in Readfield turn north on Cty Rd
W. The Evangelical Lutheran Zions Cemetery will be on the
left.

Ghost Lore

A certain grave is haunted by the spirit that rests beneath it. There
is a marble ball on top of a temple that turns every full moon. It
has never been in the same position twice.

Investigation

Of the many graves in the cemetery, it is impossible to determine
which one is allegedly haunted.

There is a granite (not marble) ball that sits atop a gravestone (not a temple). We did visit the cemetery during a full moon and have subsequently returned several times, but the ball has not changed position. Its position can be determined by the circular spot on the bottom of the sphere as it is sitting slightly off center.

Witch Road

Location: Ripon, Metomen Township, Fond du Lac County, Wisconsin
Official Name: Callan Road
Correction: Several sources erroneously list it as being in Rosendale, Wisconsin

Directions: From Ripon, go south on Hwy 44/49, turn left on Cty Rd KK, go 1.9 miles, turn right on Callan Rd. The "witch's" house will be on the left.

Ghost Lore

Approximately 50-60 years ago, a witch lived in a house on Witch Road, just outside of Rosendale, and the road has remained haunted ever since her death.

- The ghost of a little girl hides in the woods.

125

- At night, certain parts of the road are unusually dark and cold.

- After dark, the sound of trickling water can be heard near the road, though there is no stream nearby.

- The witch's dilapidated house can still be seen in the woods.

- People have seen flashing lights at the end of the road.

- White lights have been observed on the trees.

- There is a tree on the side of the road that resembles the witch.

- The ghost of a little girl has been seen hiding in the woods and peaking out from behind the trees.

Investigation

We did find the broken-down old house where the witch is supposed to have lived and found that it had fallen into a state of utter disrepair. A small brook was spotted along the road, which would account for the sound of trickling water. We spoke with an eyewit-

ness who reported seeing mysterious lights on the road. With a little imagination any number of the old trees along the road could be interpreted as resembling the traditional Halloween witch image.

Note: *The house is on private property. Please do not trespass.*

INDIANHEAD
COUNTRY
WISCONSIN

Amery Lutheran Church

Location: Amery, Polk County, Wisconsin
Proper Name: East Immanuel Lutheran Church
Address: 207 120th St., Amery, WI 54001-2901
Phone: (715) 268-2143 (Church Office Phone)
Sunday Worship: 10:00 am

Directions: Located 4 miles north of Deer Park on State Highway 46, turn left at the East Immanuel sign then 1 mile west of 46.

Ghost Lore

A phantom congregation from long ago haunts this simple country church and holds their own services late after dark.

- Hushed voices and whispers have been heard coming from

inside the walls of the building.

- Quiet voices can be heard coming from the wooden pews.

- Parishioners have heard the sounds of a congregation laughing and talking in the sanctuary, which was found to be empty.

- They have also heard the sounds of a congregation having a potluck dinner in the basement, which was empty.

Investigation

This old Norwegian church dates from 1870. Obviously, over the years many parishioners have passed on.

In 1981, the bell of the church began ringing on its own when no one was in the building. The first person to realize this startling event was the church's pastor, the Reverend Elizabeth Robinson. She heard the bell ringing while she was in the church's parsonage across the street. She investigated and thoroughly searched the building, finding no one inside. Since then, the bell has rung quite frequently on its own.

We did have the opportunity to spend the night in the church basement, but experienced nothing out of the ordinary. Parishioners and the minister seem firmly convinced of the haunting activity.

Bantley Graveyard

Location: Canton, Barron County, Wisconsin
Official Name: Pioneers Rest Cemetery

Directions: From Canton, take Cty Rd M north, turn right on 17 1/4 Ave, cross the bridge over the Pokegama Creek, the cemetery is on the right.

Ghost Lore

A certain Mr. Bantley (sometimes spelled Bantely) murdered his wife and four children and then committed suicide by hanging himself in his barn, which was located next to the graveyard.

At one time a Satanic cult used the same barn for religious rituals and used the birdbath in the graveyard for sacrifices. Blood stains can still be seen on the birdbath.

Two young boys were playing a game of tag in the graveyard after dark. A hand reached up from the ground, grabbing one of the boys by the ankles, causing him to instantly die of fright. The body of the other boy was later found outside the graveyard. The cause of death was unknown.

Numerous ghostly apparitions have been observed after dark, including the ghost of a young girl who has been observed sitting in one of the trees located inside the graveyard.

During the day, shadows will follow people who walk along the

road past the graveyard.

The Dare: If you drive over 25 mph over the bridge that crosses Pokegama Creek near the cemetery, your brakes will go out.

Note: *We don't recommend that anybody speed through here.*

Correction

The proper name of the graveyard is neither Bantely nor Bantley. It is actually "Pioneers Rest Cemetery." The confusion most likely arises because the cemetery is owned and maintained by the Bandli (notice the spelling) family. It is popularly referred to as the "Bandli Cemetery" by some of the local residents.

Investigation

Nobody by the name of Bantely or Bantley is buried in the cemetery. The Bandlis, however, do have a family plot there.

A search of the Barron County Birth, Death, and Marriage certificates turned up no records for any persons bearing the name Bantely or Bantley. Records found for Bandli family members indicated that all had died of natural causes.

We also spoke with David Bandli who confirmed that no member of his family had been murdered and that no family members had committed suicide.

We were not able to confirm the stories of Satanic cult activities in the area. The alleged birdbath is actually a planter for flowers. No bloodstains were observed.

Mr. Bandli had never heard of anyone dying while in the cemetery, thus leaving no evidence that two children died after being grabbed by some entity.

Serious flaws cast doubt on the alleged history. First, how could the hands reaching up from the ground have been observed if it was dark? Second, if the two boys witnessed the hands and later they were both found dead, how would anybody have known about the hands as there would have been no surviving eyewitnesses to report what had happened?

No ghosts were observed. No anomalous shadows were observed. We were unable to locate anybody who could offer firsthand testimony to substantiate any of the reputed phenomena.

David Bandli had heard rumors of the cemetery being haunted, but could not find an original source for the legend, nor has he ever spoken to anybody who had a firsthand experience.

We did hear an unexplained sound that was coming from a tree in the woods behind the cemetery. It closely resembled the sound of a rope tied to a tree with a suspending object swaying back and forth. Investigating the sound, we did not find two trees or branches rubbing together, and there was no breeze at the time. We shined a flashlight into the tree, but didn't see any kind of animal. Curiously, when we rapped the tree with a stick, the sound stopped and never resumed.

Ghost Island

Location: Hayward, Sawyer County, Wisconsin
Address: Barb & Bill McMahon, Golden Fawn Lodge,
8774 N. Fawn Trl., Hayward, WI 54843-6606
Phone: (715) 462-3185
E-mail: gldnfwn@cheqnet.net
Website: http://haywardlakes.com/goldenfawn.htm

Directions: From Hayward, take Hwy. B 14 miles east
to CC, right on CC 4 miles to Golden Fawn.

Ghost Lore

This cozy lakeside lodge is nestled in a small remote cove,
equipped with a beautiful view of the protected bay complete with
several islands directly on the Chippewa Flowage. Engulfed by a
forest of majestic pines, colorful maples, old oak, and superb birch
trees, this bay is said to be home to a haunted island. It is out on

the uninhabited Ghost Island that numerous guests, fishermen/women, and sightseers have encountered something truly strange. It is near this island, that a man captured a photo of a ghost with his camera. Mysterious fires have been seen on the island when no one was present. Those who stay at the resort, often claim to get an uneasy feeling while passing by Ghost Island. Mysterious lights with no known origin have been witnessed around Ghost Island.

Investigation

We spoke with Bill and Barb McMahon, who are the owners of Golden Fawn Lodge.

Bill has been fishing the flowage for over 30 years, yet he still gets a cold chill when passing by Ghost Island. Bill would often anchor his boat in a little inlet near the island that has produced some good fish in the past. However, Bill would instantaneously get the feeling that someone was watching him from the island. The hair on the back of his head would stand up with the accompaniment of an eerie chill. Bill was not certain as to the source of his uneasiness, yet he can only stay near the island for about 15 minutes. It is then, that the eeriness becomes too much for Bill, and he has to retreat home.

Bill is not the only one to experience an eerie feeling when passing by the island. The owners informed us that it was Barb who came up with the title of Ghost Island nearly 30 years ago, due to the number of guests who would report paranormal activity in the area of this mysterious island. Oftentimes guests of the lodge would inquire about who lived out on the island because they had heard voices and strange sounds echoing from the wooded area. Other guests swore that they had seen a campfire and other odd lights originating from the island. Many guests get the feeling that someone or something is watching them from the island. It should be noted that no camping is allowed on the island.

We also spoke with Bill Jr., who informed us of many of his

personal experiences near Ghost Island. Many times Bill Jr. would pass by the island and see a large orange light hovering in the woods. The light would move sporadically through the woods as though it was searching for something or someone. Bill Jr. also reported having trouble with his boat batteries near the island. It appears that new batteries in perfect working order would lose power whenever he would approach the island.

Much publicity came to the Lodge when fishing guide Al Denninger was taking a client to the Ghost Island area searching for musky. The client noticed a white floating blob of mist off in the distance. This mist appeared to have a human form to it, as the men thought they could see the outline of shoulders. Both men were baffled by what they were witnessing. The client was spooked and quickly recommended that the two men leave the area at once. Al snapped one photo of the object with his Polaroid camera. The picture seems to capture what the two men witnessed that day. Al estimated the object to be anywhere between 12-15 feet in height and stated that he had never witnessed anything like this before.

Lac Courte Oreilles Casino

Location: Hayward, Sawyer County, Wisconsin
Official Name: Lac Courte Oreilles Casino, Lodge &
Convention Center
Address: 13767W W. County Road B, Hayward, WI
54843-4184
Phone: (800) LCO-CASH or (800) 526-2274
Direct: (715) 634-5643
Fax: (715) 634-6806
E-Mail: info@lcocasino.com (General Information)
E-Mail: partyclub@lcocasino.com (Party Club
Information)
Hours: Open from 9:00 am to 2:00 am in the winter and
9:00 am to 4:00 am in the summer
Website: www.lcocasino.com

Ghost Lore

The casino is haunted because it was built on land where there used to sit a haunted farmhouse. The house was moved to a new location about a mile down the road.

Investigation

Footsteps can be heard late at night.

Employees who work the third shift have reported seeing apparitions in the casino after closing hours.

El Rancho

Location: Ladysmith, Rusk County, Wisconsin
Official Name: Best Western El Rancho Motel
Address: W8490 Flambeau Ave., Ladysmith, WI
54848-9447
Phone: (800) 359-4827 (Reservations)
Lodging Type: Limited-Service Hotel
Details: 27 rooms. Pets accepted; fee. Restaurant, bar
Check-out: 11:00 am

Directions: From Ladysmith, go 1 mile north of US 8
and Hwy 27 to the intersection of Hwy 27 and Flambeau
Ave.

Ghost Lore

The main rumor revolves around a man in a red flannel shirt that
was killed by an axe.

Allegedly the motel was built on a cemetery.

Residents of a nearby trailer court "said" they have seen this man standing in their living rooms watching them.

Investigation

We spoke with two separate employees of the El Rancho who told us that they had never heard of a man being killed at the motel.

An informant did tell us that the murder actually occurred in the 1930s at a bar called the "Bloody Bucket." The bar was located just east of where the motel is today. At that time the area was mostly rural, and the owner of the bar sold cattle on the side. One night his bartender told him that a customer wanted to meet him at the cattle barn. When he arrived at the barn, somebody murdered him with an axe. His killer was never caught; however, about six months later his bartender married his widow. Afterwards they sold the bar and quietly left town.

There is no evidence that the motel was built on a former cemetery.

According to El Rancho employees, they had never heard of any ghostly activity happening there.

We do have information from a former jailor/dispatcher indicating that back in the 1970s there was a peeping Tom who wore flannel shirts and who lived near the trailer court. Although he would quickly disappear, this was because he could "run like a deer," and not because he was a spectre. The voyeur was arrested numerous times and died several years ago.

We were unable to contact anyone from the trailer court to see if anybody alleges any recent sightings of the "peeping Tom ghost."

The former Bloody Bucket has since been completely rebuilt, and today it is a popular Ladysmith bar and restaurant with no reports of any haunting activity.

The Siren Bridge

Location: Siren, Burnett County, Wisconsin

Directions: From Hwy 35 in Siren, go east on Cty Rd B about a mile until you come to the bridge over the creek that connects Clear Lake and Long Lake.

Ghost Lore

During a Halloween blizzard, a family was driving home down County Road B when their car skidded off a bridge and overturned in a swampy stream. The parents and their young daughter were trapped in the car and all drowned.

People have reported that while driving over the bridge, they have heard the ghostly voice of a little girl come over their car radio saying, "Help me, Mommy. I can't get out!"

144

Investigation

The accident is confirmed to have happened as described.

We located two witnesses who reported this experience. In both cases they were listening to their car radio as they approached the bridge, and as they drove over the bridge their radio cut out, and they could hear the voice of a little girl pleading, "Help me, Mommy. I can't get out!" Once they crossed over the bridge, their radio returned to its regular station.

Little Valley Road

Location: Spooner, Washburn County, Wisconsin

Directions: From Hwy 63 in Spooner, go west on Cty Rd A, turn right on Cty Rd K, turn right on Little Valley Rd.

Ghost Lore

Little Valley Road is rumored to be haunted.

The Dare: If you park on the road, a phantom hearse will pull up behind you and follow you back to town.

Investigation

The story has been well known in Spooner for several years. It's not known if there was ever a death on this stretch of road or what the significance of a phantom hearse would be.

Billings Drive

Location: Superior, Douglas County, Wisconsin

Directions: From Hwy 35 in the Village of Superior, go west on Cty Rd 105 (N 61st St), Billings Dr is unmarked, but it is the second road on the right after crossing the railroad tracks.

Ghost Lore

A woman with red hair is seen walking across the road at night with her dog. She disappears into the woods.

Investigation

Billings Drive is a very scenic, unpaved road just outside of Superior. The thing that is most striking about it is how isolated it is. There are no homes for miles. To see a woman cross the road in this location, especially at night would be extremely unusual. The road is quite long, and we're not certain as to the specific location where the woman has been seen. The only information we do have is that it occurs near an old Indian cemetery, but we have been unable to locate any cemeteries on Billings Drive.

Fairlawn Mansion

Location: Superior, Douglas County, Wisconsin
Official Name: Fairlawn Mansion & Museum
Address: 906 E. 2nd St., Superior, WI 54880-3245
Phone: (715) 394-5712
FAX: (715) 394-2043
Email: info@superiorpublicmuseums.org
Website: www.fairlawnmansion.org

Ghost Lore

The home was built by Martin Pattison, the first mayor of Superior. A former housekeeper who was murdered by her husband haunts this house. The Pattison family used to sponsor Scandinavian immigrants to America by paying for their passage to this country in exchange for a period of service at their home. Martin Pattison was a kind man and usually treated the immigrants as if they were

members of the family. After completing her time of service to the
Pattisons, one servant girl married and moved away with her husband only to be murdered by him shortly thereafter. It is believed
that her spirit returned to Fairlawn Manor because that is were she
felt happiest and most secure during her short life.

The house was at one time an orphanage, and two young girls who
drowned in the pool haunt the house.

- The ghost of the murdered servant girl haunts the mansion.
  Her apparition, in 1890s dress, is frequently mistaken for the
  museum tour guides since they dress in period costume, and
  she will help lost visitors find specific displays and then vanish into thin air.

- The ghosts of two young girls has been reported in the basement playing near the swimming pool.

- People experience a cold, damp chill in the air whenever the
  ghost of the servant girl is present.

- After hours, lights have been seen in the windows on the upper
  floor.

- Faces have been seen peering out the windows.

- A figure has been seen in the tower.

Investigation

Martin Pattison, a mining and lumber baron, was not the first
mayor of Superior. He was actually the second, third, and sixth
mayor.

The 42-room mansion was constructed from 1889-1891 at a cost of
$150,000.
The Fairlawn mansion was built as the family estate of Superior's
three-time mayor Martin Pattison. He lived there with his wife
Grace and six children from 1891 to 1918.

In 1918, Grace Pattison donated Fairlawn to the Superior Children's Home and Refuge Association to be used as an orphanage. It was home to approximately 2000 children from 1920-1962. During that time the pool was empty and never used. No children ever drowned there.

There is no record of any children dying in the house; however, records from that period have been sealed by the county.

In 1963 the mansion was slated for demolition but was purchased by the City of Superior for $12,500 and has operated as a city-owned museum ever since then.

We have been unable to confirm the story of the murdered servant girl.

According to an employee of the museum, nothing paranormal has been reported during the two years she has worked there. There have been no sightings of a phantom tour guide or sprites by the pool. She believes the stories originated with a creative director of the museum who worked there several years ago and that tour guides and local residents have embellished and contributed to the stories.

She confirmed that lights have been seen in the windows after the museum has closed, but explained that guides frequently forget to shut off the lights in some of the rooms after the last tour of the day. Except for a three-week period during Christmas, the employees currently do not dress in period costume.

Note: *The current owners of the mansion deny that it is haunted and discourage people from taking the tour if they expect to see ghosts.*

NORTHEASTERN
WISCONSIN

Fifield Graveyard

Location: Fifield, Price County, Wisconsin
Official Name: Forest Home Cemetery

Directions: From Fifield, take US 70 (Oak St) east to the cemetery.

Ghost Lore

People have reported a variety of paranormal events:

- Uncomfortable feelings.

- Voices can be heard at night.

- Strange shadows.

- Orbs can be seen.

- Photos taken show orbs and ecto-mist swirling around the headstones.

Investigation

We did not experience any paranormal activity while we were in the cemetery. We did speak with a woman who informed us that her family is the caretaker of the cemetery. She stated that her grandfather passed the job onto her father and uncles, and none of them had ever mentioned any strange events taking place in the cemetery. She also stated that she had on many occasions helped dig a plot late at night for a next day burial and had never experienced anything strange.

Holy Cross

Location: Fifield, Price County, Wisconsin

Directions: From Fifield, go about 5 miles south on US 13, turn left on Holy Cross Road. Proceed to the railroad tracks. The pond is on the left side of the road.

Ghost Lore

A woman was killed by a train at the railroad crossing on Holy Cross Road and haunts the area.

- An apparition of a woman is said to be seen over the water. She has also been seen near the railroad tracks where it is said that she died. Her spirit is said to be protecting others from her fate.

- Gnomes have been spotted on the railroad tracks. When people throw rocks at the gnomes, they throw the rocks right back.

- Ghost children have been seen playing out in the field.

- Cold spots have been experienced. Even on 90-degree days.

- Mysterious lights have been observed moving through the nearby woods.

There is also a rumor that back in the 1900s there used to be a town here named Coolidge, but all the townspeople mysteriously disappeared.

Investigation

Holy Cross is the road that turns off Highway 13 between Phillips and Fifield. There is a small pond near the actual railroad tracks. No woman was spotted during our investigation. We did speak with a young child from the area who stated that many area teenagers would go stand on the tracks and feel "energy" rushing through them.

We were unable to confirm that a woman died on the road or railroad tracks.

Formerly there was a town of Coolidge, but we found nothing mysterious about its demise.

Lake of the Torches Resort Casino

Location: Lac du Flambeau, Vilas County, Wisconsin
Address: 510 Old Abe Rd., Lac du Flambeau, WI
54538-9680
Phone: (800) 25-TORCH
Website: www.lakeofthetorches.com

Ghost Lore

The casino is said to be home to several angry ghosts that will do
anything to make themselves known. Employees of this casino
report numerous encounters with ghostly apparitions. Strange
sounds are often heard by customers and employees.

Investigation

- The main hauntings are located in the bingo hall that is separated from the main casino. Employees told us of angry ghosts that would push employees from behind.

- Other employees report being pinched by an unseen attacker.

- While cleaning the facility, workers reported having their cleaning supplies moved around. Many of the employees report seeing the apparition of a woman walking through the bingo hall.

- Customers will often tell employees of their experiences of seeing a ghost and at times feeling uneasy.

History

This Northern Wisconsin Casino started as a basic bingo hall in the 1970s. Several Wisconsin tribes reached agreements with state officials that would allow for construction of bingo halls. The first bingo hall become so popular that in the 1980s the tribes wanted to expand into a casino that would encompass slots and blackjack. The tribes reached another agreement with the state and the casino, and in 1989, the casino was established in the Save Money store. The casino grew in popularity and soon outgrew its building. In 1996, the Lake of the Torches Casino opened on the beautiful shores of Pokegama Lake.

The new casino featured slots, blackjack, a hotel, and a food court. In 2002, the Woodlands Oasis water recreation center was constructed and attached to the hotel.

Lake of the Torches Resort Casino is owned by the Lac du Flambeau Band of Lake Superior Indians. Chief Keeshkemun led this band of Native Americans to the Lac du Flambeau area in 1745. The Lac du Flambeau or Lake of the Torches was taken from the practice of harvesting fish at night by torchlight.

The Lac du Flambeau Reservation was officially established by treaties in 1837 and 1842. Logging was the main industry and in later years the area became a popular tourist destination.

Photo courtesy of Todd Roll

Summerwind

Location: Land O' Lakes, Vilas County, Wisconsin

Directions: From Land O' Lakes, take Cty Rd B to West Bay Lake, turn right on Helen Creek Rd, and make a left turn, then a right turn, then another left turn. The ruins will be at the end of a dirt driveway on the right.

History

Summerwind Mansion was once a majestic home overlooking the shores of West Bay Lake. There is much speculation as to the real history of the Summerwind Mansion, as much of it is surrounded in myth and legend. What is known is that the home was built in 1916 by Robert Patterson Lamont. Lamont was the Secretary of Commerce under President Herbert Hoover and used the mansion as a summer home for his family. Lamont called the area Lilac Hills because of its natural beauty. Although many believe the paranormal activity at Summerwind did not start until the 1970s, a lot of mysterious events suggest otherwise.

It is said that Robert Lamont had many encounters with the ghosts of Summerwind and even fired his pistol at the ghosts to fend them off. Wisconsin Paranormal Researcher Todd Roll, found bullet holes in one of the doors at Summerwind. Lamont's wife Lucy was immediately displeased with the home and got a sense of uneasiness while spending time there. As time went on, Lucy became depressed and started to resent the home and her husband. Lucy tried several times to escape the home and her husband, yet each time ended in failure.

After Lamont's death, the home was sold to numerous other owners. During this time, residents of the home did not officially report any ghostly activity at Summerwind. Much of the paranormal activity at Summerwind seemed to happen to the Hinshaws. The family moved into the home during the early 1970s. The family only lived in the home for six months, yet during that time they had

numerous encounters with ghostly apparitions.

- The family reported seeing odd shapes and shadows in the hallways that appeared as though they were dancing. The family often encountered the ghost of a woman who would float back and forth through the home's large French doors.

- The family often would hear voices coming from several of the rooms, yet upon inspection, they found the rooms to be completely empty. Appliances such as the water heater and water pump would sporadically break down and then repair themselves.

- The family reported that the home's windows and doors would often open and close on their own. One morning as Arnold was approaching his car to leave for work, it spontaneously burst into flames. The cause of the fire was never determined.

Having a reputation for being haunted made it difficult for the Hinshaws to hire workers to help with the renovation of the home. The family was forced to do much of the work on their own. It was

while painting in one of the bedrooms that Arnold made a grizzly discovery. Behind a large shoe drawer in the back of the closet, Arnold discovered a secret compartment. Armed with a flashlight, Arnold slid his way into the narrow opening, only to come face to face with a rotting corpse. Frightened and repulsed, Arnold quickly jumped back away from the opening. After regaining his composure, Arnold thought that an animal must have snuck into the passage and died. He decided to go in for another look, but due to the hole being so small Arnold could not make out any details of the corpse. When Arnold's daughter Mary returned from school she volunteered to crawl into the passage. Shortly after entering the opening, Mary let out a horrifying scream and came rushing out of the hole. Mary had seen a human skull with dirty black hair along with an arm and a portion of a leg. It appears that the authorities were never notified of this discovery.

After this event, Arnold began to develop strange behaviors and displayed many symptoms of mental illness. At the same time it is also said that Ginger attempted suicide before moving away from the home. Arnold eventually was sent away for treatment of mental illness, while his wife and children moved to Granton to live

with their grandparents.

Ginger's father, Raymond Bober, looked to buy the home with the grand plan of turning it into a restaurant and inn. Bober never actually lived at the mansion as he spent his nights in an RVcamper parked outside.

Jonathan Carver

This is where the story of Jonathan Carver comes into play. Carver was an eighteenth century British explorer, said to be haunting the Summerwind Mansion. In his book, *The Haunted Northwoods,* Tom Hollatz provides great detail of Carver's life and background.

- It is said that Carver was searching for the old deed that he received from a trade with the Sioux Indians. The deed was supposed to be sealed in a box under the foundation of Summerwind.

Photo courtesy of Todd Roll

- Bober claimed that the ghost of Carver requested his help in retrieving the deed for him.

- Much of the contact between Carver and Bober was through dreams, trances, Ouija board, and automatic writings. These communications were published in Bober's book, *The Carver Effect.*

- Ginger told her father about the body that her husband had found, yet when the father went to check it out, the body was not there.

- Ginger's brother Karl began to close the windows in preparation for the upcoming rain, when he clearly heard a voice call his name, but Karl could not locate anyone in the house. Karl then heard two gun shots coming from the kitchen. As he got to the kitchen, he found the room filled with smoke and the odor of gun smoke still lingered. Yet just like with the voice calling his name, Karl found no one in the kitchen. However,

Photo courtesy of Todd Roll

this time he had found concrete proof that he was not imagining these events, as he noticed two old bullet holes in the door leading to the basement. The holes were worn and rounded as though they had been there for quite some time.

- Bober's most amazing claim was that Summerwind would change its dimensions. Bober claimed that Summerwind would shrink and expand on its own. Bober would measure a room one day, only to find its dimensions changed when he re-measured it several days later.

- Eventually Bober's dream of re-opening the home came to a disappointing end. To this day the mysterious deed that is said to exist in the home's foundation has never been found.

- The house was abandoned in the early 1980s and fell into disarray and became a target for vandalism. In 1986, investors purchased the property with the goal of re-opening Summerwind as an inn. This plan was foiled in June of 1988 when lightning set the house on fire. Today all that remains of the once majestic home is the foundation and parts of the chimney.

- There is much skepticism and doubt regarding whether or not Carver even ventured as far north as the Summerwind Mansion. There is also much debate on the legitimacy of Bober's complete account of his time there. We will leave it up to you to make up your own mind.

Note: *Summerwind is private property, and we discourage trespassing.*

Photo courtesy of Todd Roll

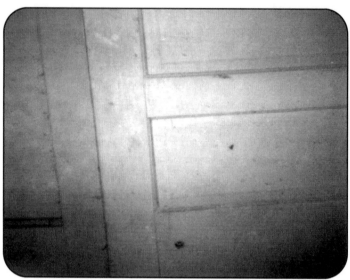

Photo courtesy of Todd Roll

The bullet holes in the door were still there when Todd Roll
visited the mansion about 20 years ago.

Photo courtesy of Todd Roll

Little Bohemia

Location: Manitowish Waters, Vilas County, Wisconsin
Address: 142 S. US Highway 51, Manitowish Waters, WI 54545-9017
Phone: (715) 543-8433

Directions: South of Manitowish Waters on US 51.

Ghost Lore

This beautiful resort lodge located off Highway 51 in Manitowish Waters is said to be haunted by the victim of notorious criminal John Dillinger. The Dillinger cabin is reported to be haunted as several guests and staff have seen apparitions while spending time at this lakeside resort. Many staff report a variety of odd things happening, from missing items to unknown voices calling out.

History

John Dillinger and his gang were known throughout the Midwest for stirring up trouble. The gang would rob banks, rob police supplies, rescue jailed friends, and any other crime that was to their liking.

In 1934, Dillinger and his gang rented some rooms at Little Bohemia. Dillinger was not alone, as Tommy Carroll, Baby Face Nelson, Three Finger Jack, and Homer Van Meter joined him. Due to the heavy firearms these men carried, along with their "gangster suits," they were immediately recognized by the owner.

The owners made the mistake of alerting the authorities by smuggling messages on matchbook covers to their relatives, who then informed the authorities. The Chicago Bureau of the Federal Justice Department was notified, and in no time, Government agents rushed to Little Bohemia. The plan was that the agents would wait for the men to come out of the lodge and then they would open fire. However, their plan was spoiled when three Civilian Conservation Corps workers decided to leave the lodge

early. The workers were mistaken for Dillinger and his crew and were fired upon. Two of them were injured and one was killed. All the gunfire alerted the gang, who immediately began to return fire at the authorities.

The gang was able to sneak out the back windows and completely vanish into the woods. The botched shootout made national headlines adding to the fame of Dillinger. The evidence of the firefight is still visible through the bullet holes that remain in the lodge.

Investigation

- We spoke with several staff of Little Bohemia who were willing to share their own stories of ghostly activity taking place at this Little Star Lake Resort.

- It is still believed that the ghost of the man killed by the authorities haunted a main sleeping cabin. The cabin has since been remodeled into a game room with a pool table.

- Before it was turned into a game room, many guests reported seeing apparitions and hearing strange voices and noises while spending the evening in this cabin.

- Many of the younger staff still report seeing ghosts and apparitions while hanging out in the game room.

- A cook reported that many things would be misplaced while he was working, yet he discounted it as being too busy to remember where items were placed.

Tula's Café

Location: Minocqua, Oneida County, Wisconsin
Address: 70 West Shopping Center, Minocqua, WI 54548
Phone: (715) 356-2847
Fax: (715) 356-3583

Ghost Lore

Years ago a man died in the restaurant. Since then, a strange mist has been reported as seen in the back hallway near where the man is alleged to have died. Also, employees report that things are moved around and not in their original positions.

Investigation

Tula's Café is located in the 70 West Building. It was originally named 70 West Café. We spoke with a manager who has been working there for over 10 years, and she stated that no man had ever died in the restaurant.

She did report that an employee claimed to see a strange mist in the hallway near the restrooms. The person is no longer an employee of Tula's and has since moved to Madison.

The manager also reported that she has found that different objects have been moved overnight. However, she pointed out that the grocery store that is the anchor of this strip mall also owns Tula's, and they often hire cleaners to come in during the night without informing the manager. Yet many employees of Tula's do believe that it is haunted. We did not experience any paranormal activity during the investigation.

Concrete Park

Location: Phillips, Price County, Wisconsin
Proper Name: Fred Smith's Wisconsin Concrete Park
For further information, write to:
Price County Forestry and Tourism Departments
Normal Building, Phillips, Wisconsin 54555
Phone: (715) 339-4505 or (715) 339-6371

Directions: On Hwy 13, 1/2 mile south of Phillips.

Ghost Lore

Among the hundreds of concrete statues, strange activities are said to take place at this popular roadside attraction. Visitors to Fred Smith's Outdoor Concrete Park report seeing statues move on their own under the cover of nightfall. Many times visitors think they actually saw real people dressed up as statues moving around.

Several residents report hearing strange noises coming from the grounds of the concrete park. Shadowy figures have also been spotted moving throughout this folk art park. Vaporous apparitions have been reported by many visitors and residents, who leave the park wondering what was real and what was a statue.

Investigation

- We spoke with several employees who had heard the stories of the park being haunted by numerous apparitions, but had not encountered the ghosts themselves.

- It appears that many of the stories regarding ghosts and moving statues originated back in the 1970s after the death of Fred Smith. It is not entirely clear whether the ghost is that of Fred Smith or someone, or something, unknown.

- No ghosts or moving statues were observed during our investigation.

History

Tucked away alongside State Highway 13, in the north woods of Phillips, is Fred Smith's collection of over 200 pieces of folk art.

Artist Fred Smith was born in 1886 to German immigrants, and was a woodsman for most of his life. In 1936, Fred built the Rock Garden Tavern with the help of two friends. In 1949, Fred retired from the lumber business due to his arthritis. Fred then became manager of the Rock Garden Tavern. Fred was married to his wonderful girlfriend May, and they had six children. Throughout the years the Smith's sold Christmas trees on their 120-acre homestead.

Fred was a self-taught sculptor who began creating his unique concrete statues in 1950 at the age of 65. His creations included soldiers, Indians, miners, and cowboys. Fred created many wildlife pieces, including a large deer jumping over a log. Fred also created many recognizable figures including Ben Hur, Abe Lincoln, Paul Bunyan, Sacagawea, and the Budweiser Clydesdales.

Fred used empty broken beer bottles from his tavern to help decorate his concrete art.

Fred's construction of the pieces consisted of building blocky characters using wooden frames for support. Fred would then wrap the piece with mink wire and layer it with concrete and other junk art materials.

In 1964, Fred suffered a stroke and had to stop creating new pieces. However, being the truly unique character he was, he still talked of making new statues up until his death in 1976. Unfortunately, shortly after his death a storm knocked down 70% of the art pieces. The Kohler Foundation stepped in to help, and the park was restored and turned over to the county.

Molly's Rock

Location: Rhinelander, Oneida County, Sugar Camp Township, Wisconsin

Directions: From Rhinelander take Hwy 17 north, turn left on Cty Rd D. At the junction with Pine Lake Rd, Molly's Rock is on the right.

Ghost Lore

A ghost named "Molly" haunts the huge rock on Pine Lake Road, outside of Rhinelander. A glowing halo has been observed above the rock.

The Dare: If somebody sits atop the rock while intoxicated, Molly will let out a scream, demand that the person "get off my rock," and then violently shove them off.

Investigation

We did observe that sunlight reflecting off the top of the rock does tend to produce a faint glow.

Although we weren't intoxicated, we did sit upon the rock and experienced nothing paranormal.

Since our visit, we have subsequently received reports that the local townspeople have demolished the rock. Apparently all that remains is a heap of rubble. People have been taking remnants of Molly's Rock home as souvenirs, but supposedly this brings ill fortune.

Rib Lake Campgrounds

Location: Rib Lake, Taylor County, Wisconsin
Official Name: Lakeview Tourist Park & Campground
AKA: Lakeview Cemetery is sometimes spelled as
"Lake View"
Phone: (800) 819-5253

Directions: From Rib Lake, take Hwy 102 west, turn
right on Lake Shore Dr, follow that until you see the
campground.

Ghost Lore

Local folklore attributes the haunting to a young boy who was
killed in an automobile accident and is buried in the cemetery next
to the campground.   During September faint moans and strange
sounds can be heard coming from the cemetery located next to the
campground.   It is said that in September the little boy will run

through the graveyard into the campground.

Investigation

- The campground is provided and maintained by the Village of Rib Lake and is directly connected to the Lakeview Cemetery. There are several campsites that are less than 15 feet away from the adjoining cemetery.

- We were unable to verify the information concerning the boy who was killed in the accident. We asked several residents of Rib Lake about the accident, but none of them were aware of it.

- Two residents did inform us that they had heard that when loggers were in the area, the lake next to the campground and cemetery was used as a dumping ground for the bodies of the dead. We were also unable to verify this information.

- We spoke with several seasonal campers who have purchased lots in the campground for their RVs, and they had never heard of the campground or cemetery being haunted. The campers also stated that they had never heard or seen anything strange over the years they have been at the campsite.

- We did spend the night at the campsite in September and found no unusual activity. We also toured the cemetery that same evening and found no paranormal activity.

- We did encounter two young individuals that were camping and reported getting an eerie feeling while walking in the cemetery.

Chicken Alley

Location: Seymour, Shawano County, Maple Grove Township, Wisconsin
Correction: Several sources erroneously list it as being in the town of Shawano

Directions: From Seymour go west on Cty Rd G, turn right on French Rd, after about 5 miles the road turns left and becomes Chicken Alley.

Ghost Lore

Are you looking for phantom trees, disappearing street signs, disembodied lights, phantom snowmobiles, ghostly voices and chickens from the grave? If you answered yes, then Chicken Alley in Seymour is the place for you. Chicken Alley is a short L-shaped road nestled into the countryside outside Shawano. Yet many bizarre occurrences have been reported on this picturesque county road. Witnesses report viewing several phantom chickens running down the street, while they are traveling down this strange county road. These chickens were easily distinguishable from real chickens, due to the fact that they could see right through them. Oftentimes these phantom chickens will vanish into thin air.

If you do find yourself driving through this area, you may want to exit your car and walk to the intersection of French Road and Chicken Alley. If you do, it is said that ghostly voices will yell at you, beckoning you to get out of the road. These voices are often interpreted as a warning signal or precautionary measure with ominous tones. However, you may have difficulty finding this eerie intersection, because many times witnesses swear that the Chicken Alley street sign disappears or is not there at all.

If you do garner the courage to travel down Chicken Alley, be sure to look for the large disfigured tree hunkering down on the side of the road. This tree is reported to be visible only on full moon nights. Many witnesses are amazed to discover that the once easily identifiable tree is not visible every trip.

Before leaving Chicken Alley, be sure to check your rearview mirror, as many residents have reported seeing mysterious disembodied lights approaching them at great speeds, only to disappear right before their eyes. The lights appear in several shapes, colors, and sizes, and have approached from all directions. During the winter, sightings of phantom snowmobiles have been reported.

Investigation

- We did stand in the middle of the intersection of Chicken Alley and French Road, and no man yelled at us.

- The Chicken Alley sign was present when we were there, as was the large disfigured tree that is reported to only come out on a full moon night. (We were not there during a full moon.)

- We did not encounter any real or phantom chickens during the investigation.

- We did not witness any bizarre lights while driving through Chicken Alley. We were unable to find any recorded cases to explain why this area may be haunted.

Calvary Cemetery

Location: Tomahawk, Lincoln County, Wisconsin

Directions: From Cty Rd S in Tomahawk turn on Cemetery Rd and follow it to the cemetery.

Ghost Lore

It is reported that strange sounds, such as whispering, babies crying, and "things" growling, are heard in the cemetery. The smell of roses and rotten flesh have also been reported. It is said that orbs have been spotted and wind is felt when there is no wind in the cemetery. Dark figures and shadows have also been reported.

Investigation

The cemetery is split into two sections. The front section contains gravestones that are flat and built into the ground. The back section of the cemetery consists of the traditional raised gravestones. Both sides of the cemetery are enclosed by wooded areas. We did not experience anything strange or out of the ordinary while we were there. However, because of the size and location of the cemetery, wind patterns were unreliable and sporadic.

PENINSULA
WISCONSIN

Shipwrecked Brew Pub

Location: Egg Harbor, Door County, Wisconsin
Official Name: Shipwrecked Brew Pub, Restaurant and Inn
Address: 7791 State Highway 42, Egg Harbor, WI 54209-9502
Mailing Address: PO Box 87, Egg Harbor, WI 54209-0087
Phone: (920) 868-2767
Toll Free: (888) 868-2767
Fax: (920) 868-9413
E-mail: shipwrecked@itol.com
Website: www.shipwreckedmicrobrew.com
Hours: Open daily, May–October, serving from 11:00 am to 10:00 pm; November–April open Wednesday through Sunday 11:00 am to 10:00 pm

Directions: Corner of Cty Rd G and Hwy 42.

Ghost Lore

This tranquil lakeside restaurant, hotel, and brewpub is convenient-ly situated right off the main road cutting through Egg Harbor. The ground floor houses the bar and restaurant, while the second floor provides several cozy sleeping rooms. With grizzly tales of Al Capone and his crew frequenting the area, along with numerous seafaring ghosts still said to inhabit the property, the drinks here are always served with a cold chill. Many customers and employees alike report seeing the ghost of a stern woman walking through the dining room. Eyewitnesses feel that this woman is checking up on the place to make sure things are still running properly. This ghost is the one most often reported at Shipwrecked, as she has been seen floating around both the upstairs and downstairs.

Other customers who have garnered enough courage to rent one of the hotel rooms, report hearing the faint crying wails of a young child, along with the sighting of a frantic young mother desperate-ly searching for her missing child.

Although the main paranormal occurrences take place inside the establishment, the attic and roof are also home to several reports of apparitions. Employees frequently see the ghost of a young man lingering in the attic. However, since the remodeling of the attic, these reports have subsided. Based on their descriptions, the ghost takes on an eerily lifelike form. In past years, many residents of Egg Harbor have called the restaurant to report the same young man walking about on the roof, yet when the owners arrived, they were unable to locate the "person" that was reported.

Not all the ghosts dwelling at Shipwrecked are so nice. Several employees and patrons have encountered a disagreeable old man. The reports of this man indicate that he may have been a lumber-jack. Thankfully for some guests, this ghost has only been seen sporadically in the last few years.

Investigation

We spoke with a member of the family who owns Shipwrecked, along with several employees and local residents, who provided us with clues to the identity of the reported ghosts.

The Shipwrecked business began in the late 1800s. During this time in Egg Harbor, lumber was the main industry. Being so close to the harbor, the town became a natural meeting place for lumber-jacks and sailors. Shipwrecked was a place to spin a good story and partake in refreshments and entertainment.

During the 1920s, the isolated location of Door County became a favorite hiding place for America's most notorious criminal, Al Capone. Al and his gang would come up to Door County from his home in Chicago. Many of the tunnels that run underneath Egg Harbor were said to provide escape routes for Al and his gang. However, do not expect to follow in Capone's footsteps, as the tunnels have long since been closed.

The current restaurant, hotel, and brewpub were not always known as Shipwrecked. In 1996, the property called Harbor Point Inn was purchased by Robert and Noreen Pollman, who are also the owners of the Door Peninsula Winery.

The woman who has been checking up on the work of current employees is believed to be Verna Moore. Verna was married and eventually divorced from Mr. Murphy Moore. Mr. Moore was one of the previous owners of the property. Verna died in her cabin located on County EE. The current owner's son was working alone in the basement one evening when he heard a woman talking. The son thought that a customer must have inadvertently wandered in behind him, so he turned around to find that no one was there. Employees feel that Verna appears as a forewarning of something bad that is about to happen. Not to worry though, as many get the feeling that Verna is a kind and gentle spirit.

The angry man that has been encountered throughout the property is believed to be a logger rumored to have been murdered at the Shipwrecked Bar during the late 1800s. The man was said to have been killed in the bar, which is no longer in the same location. We were unable to locate a name or date of death for the logger.

The crying baby is known to residents as a child of one of Capone's "girls." Apparently, the woman had the illegitimate child of Al's, which did not please Capone. The child was said to have disappeared one day and was never located. The end fate of the mother and child is still uncertain.

The ghost that is frequently seen in the attic is said to be another illegitimate son of Capone. It is rumored that the son was murdered due to his unwise choice of wanting to turn his father in to the authorities.

Institute Saloon

Location: Institute, Door County, Wisconsin
Address: 4599 State Highway 57, Sturgeon Bay, WI
54235-8844
Phone: (920) 743-1919
Email: saloon94@charter.com
Website: www.institutesaloon.homestead.com

Directions: From Sturgeon Bay take Hwy 57 north to
the intersection of Cty Rd P. The Institute Saloon is on
the northwest corner.

Ghost Lore

As one of Door County's oldest buildings, this unassuming bar and
restaurant huddled just to the side of State Highway 57 provides
residents with more than just a good burger. Although you may

inadvertently mistake this historic business for a private home, the Institute is immediately known throughout the area as a place for good fun, great food, and ghosts. Rumors of customers encountering vaporous visitors while visiting the Institute have persisted for many years. Many of these ghost reports center around the women's restroom, as it is said that a little girl encountered the ghost while alone in the restroom. Many of the bar's doors open and close without the assistance of human hands. Both staff and customers report hearing phantom voices calling out from the other side. Those who have experienced strange phenomena are convinced this historic bar is haunted by a former owner of the bar who continues to visit long after her death.

Investigation

The Institute was constructed in 1897 by John Webster Sr. and was originally used as the town's post office. The building continued to be used as a post office until the creation of free rural mail delivery. The property then changed hands several times moving from Webster to James Hanahan to John Moore to John Latanna. In 1912, the property changed hands once again, with the purchase by Joseph Petersilka. Mr. Petersilka was a well-liked and respected man around town and was able to transform the Institute into the centralized meeting place for locals and travelers. During this time, the Institute organized and promoted wrestling matches, square dances, and numerous other community events.

The bar become so popular that it started its own social club known as "the Institute 22." The bar was then sold to several different owners until it finally was purchased by Doug & Mabel Petersilka during the early 1950s. After Douglas' death in 1956, Mabel ran the whole operation by herself. Mabel eventually married again, only to have that husband pass on as well.

Mabel's daughter, Jill, sold the place to Kay Haen & Dennis Shartner in December of 1994. The team reopened the establishment shortly after.

We spoke with the owner Dennis, along with several staff and patrons, who informed us of many current paranormal happenings.

A lot of the activity centers around the ladies restroom. In 2002, a 10-year-old girl went to use the facilities alone, when she heard a voice of a woman. The startled young girl quickly retrieved her mother, who accompanied her back to the restroom. Other strange occurrences have taken place in the restroom as many other patrons report seeing a "dark shadow" along with hearing ghostly voices while alone in the restroom. While empty, the sound of the women's room stall door repeatedly opening and closing on its own can be heard throughout the bar.

The women's restroom door is not the only door to act on its own, as nearly all the doors in the bar have exhibited the same strange behavior. Various customers report being pushed off their stools by some unseen force, without the aid of alcohol.

Much of the activity seems to surround Kay and the bartender Crystal. Kay stated that one evening Crystal experienced so many anomalies that she compiled a list of grievances for her boss. While co-owner Dennis adamantly states that he has never person-ally experienced any ghostly activity, many of his staff and cus-tomers swear that Mabel is still monitoring the townsfolk at the Institute.

Rock Island State Park

Location: Rock Island, Door County, Wisconsin

Directions: Take Hwy 42 to Northport Pier, take the Washington Island Ferry (auto and passengers) to Washington Island, take Main Road or Airport Road north to Jackson Harbor Road, follow it east to Jackson Harbor, take the ferry Karfi (passengers only) to Rock Island.

Ghost Lore

This secluded island off of Death's Door is said to be inhabited by numerous ghosts from the past. Many visitors to this historic island experience ghosts in two parts of the island. Many reports come from the old Native American graveyard on the east end of the island. Strange apparitions have been spotted wandering this cemetery. Campers report odd noises and voices coming from this graveyard. The lighthouse is also said to be haunted by the ghost of a former lighthouse keeper who killed himself after several people died on a ship that crashed on his watch. Others report seeing the ghosts of small children playing near the graveyard on the west side of the island.

Investigation

- We spent the night camped next to one of the three cemeteries but had no personal experiences.

- We visited the cemetery with the graves of the two children.

- The light keeper did not kill himself, he died of natural causes in 1852. There is evidence that shipwrecks did occur on the light keeper's watch, yet it is uncertain as to whether or not anyone died. Many ships did sink during this time period, thus giving the area the name of *Porte des Morts* or Death's Door.

Potawatomi Lighthouse

- One wreck in 1902, caused seven people to be rescued. However, only four of them survived.

- The little children that reportedly haunt the cemetery died from scarlet fever as did many locals of the island.

- We did witness strange noises that came from the lighthouse. This noise sounded like someone slamming a door in the boarded up lighthouse. We heard the noise two different times and were unable to locate the source.

History

Located on the very tip of the Door County Peninsula, Rock Island is a secluded State Park surrounded by Lake Michigan. In order to get to this primitive campsite you need to catch the car ferry to Washington Island. From there you must take another ferry to Rock Island. However, do not expect any modern day conven-

The Graves of the children

iences, as no vehicles, including bikes, are allowed on this island. Rock Island is home to 40 campsites that are open to the public.

Rock Island is home to one of the most infamous lighthouses in Wisconsin. The Pottawatomie Lighthouse. The lighthouse protects the passage between Pottawatomie Island to the South and St. Martins Island to the North, and it is the oldest lighthouse in Wisconsin.

In 1834, Detroit merchants and businessmen petitioned Congress to construct a lighthouse to aid in the passage of ships sailing through the area. A 30-foot stone tower was constructed in 1836. This tower was equipped with an 11-foot lantern deck that houses an octagonal lantern. The lantern was made up of 11 oil lamps and 11 reflectors.

The first keeper of the lighthouse was David E. Corbin. Corbin, a veteran of the War of 1812, was a lifelong outdoorsman. It was Corbin's responsibility to clear a road approximately one mile long

to the south to provide access for the light. Corbin became lonely and secluded with only his horse and dog to keep him company. In 1845, Corbin received a 20-day leave of absence from the district inspector. He was to use those 20 days to find himself a wife; however, not surprisingly, Corbin failed in this mission and returned to the island alone.

In 1852, Corbin passed away at his post and was buried in the cemetery near the lighthouse.

In 1910, Chicago businessman Chester Thordason bought a large portion of Rock Island from Rasmus Hanson. Over the next few years, Thordarson acquired the rest of the island. In 1914, Thordarson restored the Jacobsen house on the east side of the island and constructed a dock. From 1927 to 1931, Thordarson constructed the boathouse and several other stone buildings on the island. During this time period, Thordarson built a total of 14 buildings, a wall, a hilltop gate, and a lookout tower on the island.

Chester and his family lived on the island for much of the year. They enjoyed working to improve the island's natural habitat. Soon after the family moved to the island, water and electricity were added to the buildings. Chester even started a greenhouse and conducted research on the plants he grew. His ability to preserve the landscape and natural habitat earned him an Honorary Master of Arts degree from the University of Wisconsin.

During the 1940s Chester and his family spent much longer periods of time on their island. It was during this productive time that Chester worked on his inventions, many of them patented. In 1944, Chester became ill and was taken care of by his family. However, when he became too sick for his family to care for him, he was transferred to a Chicago Hospital. In 1946, Chester died of heart failure in the hospital.

The University was able to purchase much of Chester's 11,000-piece, rare book collection for $300,000. Chester's two sons continued to use the island until the early 1960s. In 1965, the family sold the island to the State of Wisconsin for the amazingly low price of $170,000.

Gretchen of Range Line Road

Location: Washington Island, Door County, Wisconsin

Directions: Take Hwy 42 to Northport Pier, take the Washington Island Ferry (auto and passengers) to Washington Island, take Cty Rd W to Range Line Road.

Ghost Lore

The ghost of a former milkmaid still continues to deliver the milk to homes even after her death. Many drivers coming down Range Line Road report seeing the ghostly apparition of Gretchen. Those who have witnessed Gretchen report that she is missing her legs and seems to float down the street. Others state that there is only an eerie fog where Gretchen's legs should be.

Investigation

We did speak with several residents who have lived on the island their whole lives. They did report hearing the stories of Gretchen. One woman did remember a real person named Gretchen who lived in the area. Many recall hearing stories of Gretchen as far back as 30 years ago. We received many different reports from the residents as to the true nature of Gretchen including:

- Gretchen was a milkmaid who delivered the milk to the homes near Range Line Road. Gretchen was said to be very tall and when she died, the mortician had to cut off her legs in order to fit her into her coffin. Her loss of legs caused her to come back as the legless ghost.

- Gretchen was a milkmaid that suffered a disease that eventually twisted up her legs, and she needed to get them amputated. After her amputation she was unable to continue with her job, but after her death she resumed her job.

- Gretchen was involved in an accident when she was struck by a car and died, and she continues to deliver the milk even after her death.

- We did not encounter Gretchen as we investigated Range Line Road.

- We were unable to locate any recorded story of Gretchen and the case still remains open.

Nelsen's Hall

Location: Washington Island, Door County, Wisconsin
Official Name: Nelsen's Hall Bitters Restaurant & Pub
Address: RR 1 Box 19, Washington Island, WI 54246-9706
Phone: (920) 847-2496
Toll-free: (877) NELSENS or (877) 635-7367
Email: bitterspub@itol.com
Website: www.washingtonisland.com/nelsens

Directions: Take Hwy 42 to Northport Pier, take the Washington Island Ferry (auto and passenger) to Washington Island, take Cty Rd W to Main Rd. Nelsen's will be on the left.

Ghost Lore

Settled on beautiful Washington Island, this ranch-style bar and restaurant is said to house the ghost of a former owner. Patrons report encountering strange apparitions while in the restroom. Bartenders are said to have heard mysterious voices calling their name. Phantom footsteps are often heard while staff is cleaning up. A mischievous ghost, hell-bent on playing its favorite music, has been spotted in the bar.

History

Danish immigrant Tom Nelsen constructed the hall in 1899 to serve as a community center and social retreat for residents and visitors. The hall has taken on several personalities throughout the years, including serving as an ice cream parlor, dentist office, pharmacy, movie theatre, and of course, a tavern. It even served as the headquarters for the illustrious Bitters Club. The back bar was brought in from a Michigan sailing ship in 1850. The bar that is now adjacent to the main hall was constructed in 1902.

Bitters liquor became associated with the hall through former owner, Tom Nelsen. Tom established the custom of drinking Angostura Bitters as a stomach tonic. Tom was said to have consumed a pint of bitters a day throughout most of his 90 years. According to Tom, it was the secret to his good health.

At the start of prohibition, Tom applied for a pharmacist's license in order to dispense his stomach tonic to the local residents. As a pharmacist, Tom was able to continue selling his 90 proof Angostura Bitters tonic and thus his bar was able to remain open. Tom's creativity resulted in Nelsen's Hall becoming the oldest, legally, continuously operating saloon in the state of Wisconsin.

When you visit Nelsen's Hall, be prepared to partake in the tradition of doing a shot of Bitters, as each year more than 10,000 people become a card carrying member of the Bitters club. Members of this club, including ourselves, come from nearly every state, along with many individuals from foreign counties. Because of the tradition, more Bitters is consumed per capita at Nelsen's Hall than any other place in the world. Visiting the unique bar you will quickly find out why *Men's Journal Magazine* listed it as one of the 50 best bars in America.

Investigation

- Speaking with co-owner Doug, we were informed of numerous haunting experiences that have taken place at this pub. Many staff and customers believe this historic pub is still inhabited by its former owner, Tom Nelsen.

- Often after the bar has closed for the evening, the staff will report phantom footsteps leading up the stairs to Doug's apartment. This is the same area where Tom Nelsen passed away.

- During a wedding that took place at the hall, a guest went into the women's bathroom only to come out extremely frightened. She reported seeing an apparition staring at her while she was trying to use the facilities.

- Bartender Robin was working one evening when she heard someone clearly ask for a glass of water; however, when she turned around, she was shocked to discover no one was there. Many evenings while tending bar, Robin swears that she has caught a glimpse of Tom's ghost passing through the establishment.

- Fellow bartender Dave was dropping off some money when he heard a heavy door slam on its own without the aid of a human hand.

- A female bartender was closing up one evening while Doug was finishing some work in the kitchen, when the radio mysteriously turned on by itself. The odd part of this experience was that while the radio never changes from the rock station it is tuned to, that evening the radio was playing country music.

- During the springtime, Doug was attempting to clean the windows of the hall, as he had done countless others times, when the window came crashing down on his hand chopping off a part of his finger. Based on personal experiences, Doug is not ruling out the possibility of the ghost being responsible for this "accident."

SOUTH CENTRAL WISCONSIN

Highway 12 Hitchhiker

Location: Baraboo, Sauk County, Wisconsin

Directions: Hwy 12 in Baraboo.

Ghost Lore

Travelers have reported seeing a male hitchhiker dressed in a green jacket. He is described as having black hair and a beard. The hitch-hiker is passed, only to be seen again one mile down the road. If someone stops to pick him up, he disappears and cannot be found.

Investigation

We were unable to find any witnesses that have actually seen this man. Hwy 12 is a very long stretch of road. We traveled this road and did not encounter this or any other hitchhiker. Being that there is no date, time, specific location, or personal account, the case is difficult to prove or disprove.

Weary Bridge

Location: Evansville, Rock County, Wisconsin
Correction: Several sources erroneously list the road as being in the town of Stoughton

Directions: From Evansville, take US 14 west about 2 miles, turn right on N Tuttle Rd, turn right on W Weary Rd. At the first curve is Weary Bridge.

Ghost Lore

Supposedly a death occurred at the bridge, resulting in it being haunted. There is more than one version of events.

- One story is that a young man was "car surfing" —standing on the top of a moving vehicle—when he fell off at the Weary Bridge as they were turning, and he was killed.

- Another story is that a carload of joyriding high school students were killed when they were speeding around the corner and accidentally drove off the bridge into the water.

- Yet another story is that the body of a young boy was found hanged on the bridge. Whether it was suicide or a lynching is unknown.

People describe all kinds of strange things here.

- Mechanical problems with their vehicles.

- Shadowy figures that dart across the road or follow people.

- Finding unexplained scratches on their bodies.

- Imps—small demons—hiding in the trees.

- Strange orbs of light.

- A mysterious green glow at the end of the road.

- Phantom trains, cars, and motorcycles.

The Dare: If you park your car on the bridge at night and shut off the engine, it will fail to restart.

Investigation

We have been unable to find any evidence of any deaths on this stretch of road.

There are railroad tracks on the north end of Weary Road. Whether the phantom trains are seen or heard, we are not sure.

The stretch of Weary Road that leads to the bridge has a beautiful canopy of trees that creates a cathedral effect; however, as soon as the sun begins to set, these same trees begin to take on an ominous appearance.

The polluted stream beneath the bridge.

Weary Road

Location: Evansville, Rock County, Wisconsin
Correction: Several sources erroneously list the road as being in the town of Stoughton

Directions: From Evansville, take US 14 west about 2 miles, turn right on N Tuttle Rd, turn right on W Weary Rd. At the first curve is Weary Bridge.

Ghost Lore

Weary Road was supposedly named for Old Man Weary who lived on the road many years ago. Although most people agree that he died by fire, there is a great deal of disagreement over the events leading up to that fire.

- Old Man Weary was supposedly a wealthy land baron who

owned most of the land surrounding Evansville. He was a greedy old man who lived in a huge estate on Weary Road with a staff of servants. The town of Evansville hated him and his family. One account has it that some of the townspeople conspired together and put him to death by tying him to his bed and razing his mansion. A different version is that he murdered his own family then set his home on fire and died in the blaze.

> **"It was a weary, weary road**
> **That led thee to the pleasant coast,**
> **Where thou, in his serene abode,**
> **Hast met thy father's ghost"**
>
> THE INDIAN GIRL'S LAMENT
> by William Cullen Bryant
> 1824

- A second story is that Old Man Weary was a kindly old gentleman who loved children and would frequently entertain them in his humble abode. The townspeople, however, believed he was a pedophile, so they torched his house, not realizing that he was innocent. Unbeknownst to them, there were children in the house with him who also perished in the fire.

- A third tale is that Old Man Weary was a deranged psychopath who hated it whenever teenagers would trespass on his property. Eventually he began to murder them, and this went on for some time. Finally, some local teens decided to take matters into their hands, and killed him by burning down his house. After that, high school students would hang out and party on Weary Road near the spot where his house used to be. It is believed that Old Man Weary haunts the road and seeks revenge, killing teenagers every chance he gets.

The Dares: If you park your car on the bridge, and shut off your headlights, the ghost of Old Man Weary will appear; if you look in your rearview mirror, you will see him, and each time you look back, he will be closer to your car.

Investigation

After doing some research, we found that there actually was a Weary family that lived on Weary Road.

Lewis Weary was born in Akron, Ohio, on May 12, 1839. He was married at the age of 25 and had four children. His wife died on May 31, 1877. Lewis was spoken of as an indulgent parent and remembered by many for the acts of kindness he showed. He was sick for six months and finally succumbed on October 24, 1918.

Charles Henry Weary, the son of Lewis, was born on September 12, 1865. On December 18, 1888, he married Elva Josephine Story, and they had only one child, Russell Lewis, born in 1892 on their wedding anniversary. In 1902, Charles purchased the Frank Van Patten farm on what is today known as Weary Road just outside of Evansville.

Russell Lewis Weary was a graduate from the Evansville Seminary. He married Margaret Holden on August 18, 1919 and they lived on the Weary farm with his parents. After his father Charles died on December 28, 1933, Russell continued to live on the farm with his wife and mother and work as a dairy farmer. In 1945, they sold the property and moved to 23 South First Street in Evansville. At that time, Russell retired from farming and was employed in Evansville for several years in the Grange Store and later at Baumgartens Foods Store. He was an upstanding member of the First Baptist Church in Evansville, where he served as a deacon and in other church offices for many years. On October 14, 1947, his mother Elva passed away, after being critically ill for one week with a heart ailment.

Russel and Margaret only had one child, Lois. In April of 1971, they moved to Blacksburg, Virginia. Russell died on July 30, 1973; Margaret eventually followed him in death on April 2, 1989.

Lewis, Charles, Elva, Russell, and Margaret are all buried in the family plot in the Maple Hill Cemetery in Evansville.

The facts reveal that most of the rumors about Weary Road are completely false.

- The Wearys neither molested children nor killed teenagers.

- They were upstanding members in their church and community.

- None of them died in a fire.

- They lived on a simple farm, not in a wealthy mansion.

- The house was on the north end of Weary Road, not on the south end near the bridge.

- The section of road with the line of trees and the bridge is new and did not even exist when the Wearys lived out there.

- Their house never burned. In fact, it is still there on Weary Road. The house where they lived in town is also still there.

Shadow Demon

Location: Greenwood Cemetery, Nekoosa, Juneau County, Armenia Township, Wisconsin

Directions: From Nekoosa, take Cty Rd AA south, turn left on Plank Hill Ln, which later becomes 26th Ave N. The cemetery will be on the left.

Ghost Lore

In October of 1961, three teenagers parked their car at the entrance of the Greenwood cemetery just as dusk was approaching. Suddenly they saw the iron gate swing open by itself, and this was followed by the sound of howling that was seemingly coming from several corners of the cemetery. Getting out to investigate, they spied a six-foot-tall shadowy figure near one of the tombstones. They watched as it appeared and disappeared behind several different headstones. Later it was stomping on a fresh grave, and its

howls turned into screams.

The terrified, young men jumped back into their car and drove to a local bar where they told a couple of their friends about their experience. The friends were skeptical yet intrigued. The five of them took two cars and drove back to the cemetery. Shining their headlights into the graveyard revealed nothing out of the ordinary. They got out of their cars and walked through the gate that was still open. In the corner of the cemetery was a storage shed where the groundskeeper kept his equipment. The men saw the shed door open up, and they could see the shadowy figure inside. When it began to howl, they bolted for their cars and sped away.

Investigation

We visited the Greenwood cemetery and were able to verify the existence of the iron gates, the storage shed, and a grave from 1961.

Case Courtesy of Richard Hendricks

The grave of Elizabeth Nelson (1886-1961)

Church Road Cemetery

Location: Portage, Columbia County, Wisconsin
Official Name: Saint Michael's Cemetery

Directions: From Hwy 16 in Portage, take Cty Rd O, turn right on Church Rd, the cemetery is on the left.

Ghost Lore

It is rumored that a young girl has been spotted hanging from a tree. Dark shadows have also been reported moving from headstone to headstone at night.

Investigation

If any cemetery looks like the stereotypical haunted cemetery, this one is it. This cemetery is nestled on the end of a dead end road.

The cemetery is approximately 60 yards off the main road through a small grass field. Our investigation turned up nothing conclusive, yet an odd smell was sensed. The cemetery also houses many trees with limbs that hang down which could conceivably be mistaken for a rope. No girl was spotted and no moving shadows were encountered.

Wisconsin Street

Location: Portage, Columbia County, Wisconsin

Directions: Take US 51 to Portage, it becomes Wisconsin St.

Ghost Lore

On Wisconsin Street in Portage, at about 9:00 p.m., you might see a lady, dressed in the style from the early 1900s, walking on the sidewalk with a stroller. But as you get closer, the image disappears.

Investigation

Wisconsin Street is a very long stretch of road that is comprised of both commercial and residential housing structures. It runs through the heart of the populated downtown to the countryside.

We spoke with several downtown employees who work on Wisconsin Street. None of them had ever heard the story. In addition, nobody had ever seen a woman matching the description of the one from the story.

We traveled a long stretch of the road from 8:30 p.m. to 9:30 p.m. and did not witness any woman pushing a stroller.

Other than the description of the woman's 1900's style of dress, we lack specific details about her height, race, color of hair, etc.

We also do not know where this woman was spotted, as it seems unlikely numerous people would not have seen her if she was spotted downtown or in the residential area. A woman dressed in 1900's garb along with a large 1900's stroller would be hard to miss. There are no sidewalks as you continue on Wisconsin Street towards the country, which eliminates that area since, according to the story, she is seen on a sidewalk.

Having a specific time for the "woman" to appear is a sign that the story is local folklore. Does she appear at 8:50, 9:10, or only at 9:00 p.m.? This haunting is classified as unlikely, but possible.

Dungeon of Horrors

Location: Wisconsin Dells, Columbia County, Wisconsin
Official Name: Bill Nehring's Dungeon of Horrors
Address: 325 Broadway, Wisconsin Dells, WI 53965-1506
Phone: (608) 254-2980

Ghost Lore

- The building used to be a Ford garage. The owner committed suicide there by shooting himself.

- The Ford garage had gas pumps in front, and somebody accidentally blew himself up while putting gas in his motorcycle.

- There used to be a mortuary next door that may have originally been part of the same building.

- Employees have seen an apparition of an older man with glasses, who disappears.

- An apparition carrying an axe has been seen following people.

- Cold spots.

- Glowing orbs.

- A partial hand has been observed to materialize then disappear.

- People have felt breathing on their shoulder when nobody was there.

- People have been grabbed by invisible hands and hit with invisible objects.

- On one occasion the owner felt something on his shoulder and could hear static or crackling in his ear; at that same time, the employees saw a glowing, orange apparition. One worker shouted, "There it is!" At the moment the entity moved off and dissipated, the static sound ended.

- There was an alcoholic artist who died in an apartment next door several years ago.

Investigation

We spoke with the owner, Bill Nehring, who confirmed that in the late 1950s or early 1960s the owner of the Ford garage killed himself one morning with a shotgun just as the employees were coming in the front door.

Mr. Nehring confirmed that the haunting activity has been going on for some time and that he has had a difficult time keeping employees because of this activity. According to him, the activity seems to peak during the month of August every year; also during rainy, overcast days. He estimates that over the past 24 years he has owned the place, about 80% of his employees have had some kind of paranormal experience.

Showboat Saloon

Location: Wisconsin Dells, Columbia County, Wisconsin
Official Name: Captain Brady's Showboat Saloon
Address: 24 Broadway, Wisconsin Dells, WI 53965-1546
Phone: (608) 254-2980

Ghost Lore

At one time there was a girl named "Molly" who lived above the saloon and has haunted the building ever since her death. All of the haunting activity is benign and usually occurs after 3:00 a.m.

- The upstairs doors will open and close by themselves.
- When people are cooking in the upstairs kitchen, the ghost will play around with the appliances.

- Apparitions of people dressed in turn-of-the-century clothing have been seen in the mirrors in the saloon.

- Strange voices have been heard near the saloon stage.

- Cold spots are felt in the cellar.

- Kegs of beer are moved around in the cellar.

- Feelings of nausea and sudden anxiety in the cellar.

Investigation

We spoke with a bartender who had worked in the saloon for the past two years, and he indicated that during that time he had never experienced anything unusual. We also spoke with the previous owner, Michael Showalter, who confirmed the haunting activity.

At this point in our investigation we have been unable to verify that there was a Molly who was a tenant in the upstairs apartment.

SOUTHEASTERN WISCONSIN

Root River Bridge

Location: Caledonia, Racine County, Wisconsin

Directions: From Racine, take Hwy 38 north to the Caledonia/Oak Creek border near the Root River.

Ghost Lore

Back in the 1970s, a young boy was playing in the woods near the bridge and accidentally drowned in the Root River.

Late at night, people have seen his ghostly image walking in the spooky woods near the river bank.

Investigation

On the northeast side of the river, there is a parking area on the side of the road. From there, a hiking trail leads down to the river. The forest is lush and filled with huge trees that almost appear to have anthropomorphic features, complete with menacing faces and hands with long fingers ready to grab the unwary visitors who hike this path.

The muddy waters of the river give no clues as to how deep it might be or what might lie beneath it. The area would be a creepy place for a ghost encounter.

Glenbeulah Graveyard

Location: Glenbeulah, Sheboygan County, Wisconsin
Official Name: Walnut Grove Cemetery

Directions: From either Fond du Lac or Sheboygan, take Hwy 23 towards Glenbeulah, go north on Cty Rd A, which becomes W Main St, turn right on Swift St, right on Appleton St, and left on Walnut St, which leads to the Walnut Grove Cemetery.

Ghost Lore

- A man hanged himself in the Glenbeulah Graveyard. Later, his decapitated head rolled down the hill and into the town. Now his ghost can be seen wandering through the graveyard after midnight.

- People have reported seeing apparitions, including strange reddish/white people.

- One of the graves will actually glow in the dark and strange lights will appear around the graves.

- People have heard strange noises.

- A pair of shoes has been seen to materialize on a grave.

- Several of the graves mysteriously split apart down the middle.

- Back in the woods is a secluded, secret house where somebody lives.

- The graveyard was featured on *Unsolved Mysteries* a few years ago, and they were able to document the ghostly activities in the cemetery.

- At one time, this was considered to be the third most haunted place in the world.

Investigation

This secluded, and difficult to find, cemetery is one of the most talked about in Wisconsin.

It was never featured on *Unsolved Mysteries*, and it was never ranked as the third most haunted place in the world.

We found no evidence that anybody hanged themseves in the cemetery.

Ferrante's Grafton Hotel

Location: Grafton, Ozaukee County, Wisconsin
Address: 1312 Wisconsin Ave., Grafton, WI 53024-1959
Phone: (262) 376-9290

Ghost Lore

- People hear footsteps following them in the basement.
- Music has been heard playing upstairs when nobody was there.
- Cabinets open and close by themselves.
- Ghostly figures have been seen in the basement.

Investigation

Ferrantes Grafton is an Italian-American restaurant located in the Historical Grafton Hotel in downtown Grafton. The Grafton Hotel has not been a working hotel for over 30 years. The guestrooms have been converted into private banquet rooms.

The manager confirmed that strange things were happening in the building. Although they believed the hotel/restaurant was haunted, they did not mind coexisting with what they considered to be friendly spirits.

The employees reported that they have witnessed unexplained events in the building. The day before we interviewed them, a huge crucifix had fallen off the wall for no explainable reason.

Eagle Road Cemetery

Location: Juneau, Dodge County, Clyman Township, Wisconsin
Official Names: Evangelical Church Cemetery or Tabor Cemetery

Directions: From Juneau, take Cty Rd M south, turn left on Eagle Rd. The cemetery is about one-half mile down the road on the right.

Ghost Lore

• Apparitions have been seen in the graveyard at night.

• Cold spots and breezes are felt even on warm summer nights.

• Epiphanies of the Virgin Mary have been seen.

- People have returned from the cemetery with blood on their hands and arms (stigmata?).

Investigation

At one time, there was an Evangelical Church here, and the cemetery belonged to that congregation. This denomination, founded by Jacob Albright in 1807, is not Catholic, so reports of epiphanies of the the Virgin Mary and possible stigmata seem out of place.

La Belle Cemetery

Location: Oconomowoc, Waukesha County, Wisconsin

Directions: From Oconomowoc, take Hwy 16, which becomes E Wisconsin Ave, go right on N Fowler St, turn right on N Oakwood Ave, cross the bridge, turn right on E Grove St, cross the second bridge, follow the road into the cemetery.

Ghost Lore

In the cemetery, there is a large, stone monument of a young woman standing near a cross.

- Sometimes the hands of the statue will drip blood.

- People have seen an apparition of the girl walking from the statue and drowning herself in nearby Lac La Belle.

- People have seen the statue come to life, walk down the stone steps, and walk into Fowler Lake.

- The statue has led to mysterious deaths, blindness, and other misfortunes.

Investigation

There is, indeed, a granite statue of a young girl, perhaps an angel, holding a bouquet of Easter Lilies. She stands in mourning next to a large granite cross. Located directly in front of the statue is the plot for the Nathusius family. Buried there is the father Carl (1830-1921), mother Louise (1832-1917), brother Wilhelm (1865-1945), and daughter Carolina (1865-1952).

Fowler Lake is, indeed, within walking distance and only a few yards from the statue; however, there is no reason to believe that either the mother or the daughter committed suicide by drowning. Lac La Belle is farther away, and most likely, people are confusing

it with Fowler Lake.

Neither the mother nor the daughter were young women at the time of their deaths. The mother died at age 85 and the daughter died at age 87.

As far as the alleged stigmata, an examination of the hands on the statue showed no indication of any kind of blood stains or abnormality. People who visit the grave sometimes place coins and other objects into the hands.

History

The Archie Monument & Stone company in Oconomowoc erected this monument in the La Belle Cemetery in the 1940s for the Nathusius family. In fact, the Nathusius family used to own a tavern right behind their monument store. Part of the payment for the monument involved free food and drinks in the tavern for many years thereafter, as bartering was more common in those days. A statue like that would cost about $200,000.00 today, and it is without a doubt the most expensive monument in the La Belle Cemetery.

The Nathusius monument is an original piece of artwork produced by an unknown Italian sculptor from Barre, Vermont. It was carved from what is known as Barre (pronounced like "bury") Granite.

Veterans Park

Location: Oostburg, Sheboygan County, Wisconsin
Address: 1140 Park Ave., Oostburg, WI 53070-1163

Ghost Lore

A few years ago, there was a drifter who drowned in the creek.

People have reported seeing a man walking the banks of the creek, and when he is approached, he seems to walk into the creek and disappear.

Investigation

We are investigating to find out if someone did actually die in the creek. However, it should be noted that the creek that runs through the side of the park is extremely narrow and shallow. Even at a high point of heavy rain, the creek does not seem large enough for a man to drown. This person would have had to actually fall face down in this creek in order to have drowned.

Others report hearing strange noises coming from the creek. These noises are a mixture of animal and human cries.

ALLEGED PORTAL TO HELL

Hotel Hell

Location: Maribel, Manitowoc County, Wisconsin

Directions: From Interstate 43 take Hwy 147 east, turn right on Cty Rd R, the Maribel Caves Hotel will be on the right.

Ghost Lore

- There have been a number of sightings of a figure standing at one of the windows peering out.

- Many people have reported hearing strange noises such as voices, screams from the basement, footsteps, ringing bells, rolling wheels, and things moving around upstairs.

- The odor of sewer gases can be smelled in the bathrooms.

- Some have claimed to have seen objects levitate and move.

- In the basement, people have reported having feelings of being threatened.

- On the third floor, people have reported feeling cold hands applying pressure to their back.

- Books found upstairs have reportedly burst into flames.

- Apparitions have reportedly been seen on the front lawn and sitting on the side of the road.

- The ghost of the little boy who died nearby in the bottling factory fire has been seen playing on the roof.

- The building glows brightly during the new moon.

- Blood has been seen on the walls.

- The building burned three times and each time on the exact same date. It was rebuilt twice. The first fire was in the 1920s. The last fire was in 1930 and everybody died in their sleep. Skeletal remains of some of the victims can still be found on the third floor and in the basement.

- Years ago, one of the hotel guests went psycho and killed everybody in the hotel during a mass-murder frenzy, and afterwards he committed suicide.

- The spirits of those killed in the hotel have lingered in the building. This spiritual activity attracted a group of local black witches who conducted secret rituals to curse the hotel. In the process, they opened up a portal to Hell through an old fountain in the front of the hotel. This unleashed a horde of evil spirits that terrorized the town of Maribel. Fortunately, a white witch came to the rescue, sealing off the portal and confining the demons to the boundaries of the hotel and the surrounding yard.

- It used to be a spa in the late 1800s for movie stars.

- During the prohibition, the hotel was owned by Al Capone.

- It served as a hideout for Al Capone, and he ran a moonshine business out of the hotel and the water bottling company next door.

- Underground passageways, built beneath the hotel during the bootlegging days, contain the lost treasures of Al Capone and John Dillinger.

- A little boy was playing on the roof of the bottling factory and was killed when it caught on fire.

The Dare: If you shine your flashlight at a second story window, a ghost will flash a light back at you.

Corrections: The correct name is "Maribel Caves Hotel," and it was named after the neighboring Cherney Maribel Caves. Ghost web sites erroneously spell the town as "Maribell" and the county as "Manitowac." They also mistakenly refer to it as "Motel Hell," but it is more popularly known to the local residents as "Hotel Hell." Some sources list the original owner as "Steinbrecher," but it is actually "Steinbrecker."

Investigation

- The hotel has burned only once, in June of 1985. The cause was unknown. Nobody was killed in the fire. There are no skeletal remains.

- There is no evidence of a mass murder and suicide at the hotel.

- There is no evidence of a portal to Hell.

- Al Capone never owned the hotel.

- For a while it did operate as a health spa where people could benefit from the therapeutic effects of the local mineral spring water, but cinema was in its infancy in the late 1800s; consequently, it would not have been frequented by movie stars.

- Austrian immigrant, Charles Steinbrecker, designed the hotel to resemble health spas he saw in Innsbruck, Austria. He died in 1892 before it could be built. Eventually, it was built in 1900 by his sons, Father Francis Steinbrecker and Eugene Steinbrecker. It was built with limestone from the area. Thirty masons, commissioned by Father Francis of St. Mary's Catholic Church in Kaukauna, completed the project in four months. The Steinbrecker family ran it as a health spa hotel and retreat for clergy. When Father Francis died in 1927, the hotel experienced a change in clientele, which included bootleggers, mobsters, and prostitutes. It went through several ownership changes until it was purchased in 1986 by the present-day owner Bob Lyman.

- At one time, a bottling plant was built next to the hotel. The Maribel spring water was sold to fine restaurants and hotels in Milwaukee, Chicago, and other cities.

- It may have been a hideout for Al Capone, and it is possible he ran moonshine out of it. The hotel was the midway point between Chicago and Al Capone's hideout in Couderay, Wisconsin. The bottling company would have made the perfect cover for his moonshine operation.

- Although Al Capone and John Dillinger may have frequented the hotel, there is no evidence of secret passageways or hidden treasures.

- There is no evidence to support the story of a little boy dying in a fire at the bottling factory.

- We spoke with one witness who, on a dare, had spent the night in the dilapidated building. She reported hearing voices, footsteps, and things moving around.

- Currently the owners and the county are considering whether they should renovate or raze the building.

Note: *This is private property under constant surveillance. Observe it from the road, but do not trespass.*

Brumder Mansion Bed & Breakfast

Location: Milwaukee, Milwaukee County, Wisconsin
Address: 3046 W. Wisconsin Ave., Milwaukee, WI
53208-3950
Phone: (414) 342-9767 (Reservations)
Toll Free: (866) 793-3676
Email: brumdermansion@wi.rr.com
Website: www.brumdermansion.com

Ghost Lore

- The Gold Suite is said to be haunted by the ghost of a woman.

- Many guests have reported seeing a ghost of a woman in the basement where the theatre is.

- The ghost is said to dislike dogs in "her" room.

History

George Brumder, a prominent Milwaukee business leader, built this majestic brick home in 1910 for his eldest son George Jr. In the late 1800s, George Brumder came to Milwaukee where he purchased an ailing publishing company. He quickly turned the business around and proceeded to make a large fortune publishing numerous German language newspapers, Bibles, and sheet music in the community. The family later branched out into banking and manufacturing.

Since the Brumders moved on, the mansion has been a boarding house, a parsonage, and activity center for the Lutheran Church. Designed in the English Arts & Crafts style, it blends Victorian, Gothic, and Arts & Crafts elements. Various rooms had been converted into individual offices, a stage was added to the lower level "ballroom" and a psychedelic youth chapel was built on the second floor. The Theatre, which was originally a billiard room, was a coffee house and live music venue called The Catacombs in the '60s. When the Hirschis bought the home from the church in 1997, it was in a state of disrepair and rather institutional in appearance. Upon

taking ownership, Carol Hirschi revitalized this grand old mansion, bringing back the look and feel of the Victorian era. The bed and breakfast opened in April of 1998.

Investigation

We spoke with the current owner, Carol Hirschi, who told of the following experiences at the Brumder mansion:

- A psychic, without any prior knowledge of the room being haunted, spent the evening in the Gold Suite and came down for breakfast the following morning. The psychic reported having dreams of the room being haunted by a woman.

- Patrons report seeing the ghost of Aunt Pussy while occupying the Gold Suite. Aunt Pussy was a formal resident of the mansion.

- The main doorbell would not function whenever a guest came

Photo courtesy of Richard Hendricks

to the door. The doorbell would only work for guests when it was set on a specific ring tone; however, the doorbell worked at any other time for all of the employees. The doorbell was such a problem that a phone had to be installed outside the main entrance for the use of prospective guests.

- The owner went to check on the Gold Suite after it had not been rented in several days and discovered fresh wet blood in the bathtub. She was unable to explain the origin of the blood.

- A guest was walking downstairs admiring the theatre when she noticed what appeared to be a ghost of a woman. The ghost was wearing an old green dress with her hair pulled back reminiscent of an early 1900's wardrobe.

- Those who have had dogs in the Gold Suite with them have reported having strange dreams of a woman that seemed to dislike dogs and threatened to harm the dog. Guests awake with the overwhelming urge to remove the dog from the room in order to avoid harm.

Photo courtesy of Richard Hendricks

JFK Prep

Location: Saint Nazianz, Manitowoc County, Wisconsin

Directions: From Saint Nazianz, go south on S 4th Ave (Cty Rd A). JFK will be on the right (west).

Ghost Lore

This former Catholic prep school is shrouded in mystery, as numerous conflicting stories of its origin and haunting pass from the lips of curious parties. Today, the series of dilapidated buildings are in disrepair as many windows are busted out, the walls are covered with graffiti, and nearly all of the buildings are so rundown, just walking through them proves a safety challenge.

The series of buildings housed on 38 acres are known to many people as JFK Prep, St. Nazianz, Salvatorian Seminary, and the Leadership Academy. However, regardless of its title, many people believe that the ghosts of former residents still lurk about the buildings. Tales of physical and sexual abuse become theories speculating on the origins of the hauntings. Many believe the school was constructed in the early 1900s by a sect of Germany Catholics who came over to the United States to practice pedophilia, incest, and homosexuality.

Wild tales of ghosts, demons, and other strange anomalies persist still today. It is said that numerous people have encountered the ghosts of former children who were abused and beaten and whose spirits have chosen to remain on their old school grounds. One of the buildings is home to the Satan room, where is it said that a priest encountered Satan and the school officials had to seal off the room to protect the children and staff.

Those brave enough to venture onto the building grounds have reported being overcome with fright and a foreboding sense of fear and doom. Visitors have reported getting a severe headache the minute they cross onto the property. Curious visitors also report seeing apparitions throughout the buildings, and many of these visitors report hearing the sounds of children playing as they make

their way through the property.

Another main rumor is that a former nun, who used to torture and abuse the boys, took her own life at the end of a rope. The reports state that she ended her life after killing two boys and became scared of being caught and punished. The nun is said to continue to haunt the grounds and the graveyard where she is buried. Another tale of the nun revolves around the suicide of a young female student who hanged herself in the auditorium while attending JFK Prep during the 1970s. The girl claimed she was haunted by the ghost of the deceased nun.

Investigation

Rev. Ambrose Oschwald brought his religious followers from Baden, Germany to the location now called St. Nazianz. The Reverend was seeking refuge for his religious followers. The rumors of pedophilia, incest, and homosexuality have not been substantiated.

Once the Reverend was in Wisconsin, he purchased a home, while his followers purchased nearly 400 acres of land for approximately $14,000. Oschwald built the first house of worship in 1854, and was gaining notoriety throughout the area, forcing him to construct a convent and Franciscan monastery. By 1864, Oschwald's following had reached 56 members and 48 families who were not officially members of the colony. The colony was then known as the Society of the Divine Savior.

We were unable to find any evidence leading to the death of a former nun. The graveyard that exists in the back of the property is exclusively for the priests as no nuns are buried there. There was an orphan asylum for girls and a hospital, yet neither lasted very long as both had been removed by 1900. We have found no evidence of a young girl hanging herself; however, we are certainly not ruling out this possibility.

Rev. Ambrose Oschwald passed away in 1873 and was buried in a sepulcher near the old Ambrosius Church. He was eventually moved to the sepulcher closer to the Loretto Shrine. During that same year, Archbishop Frederick Katzer of Milwaukee came up to St. Nazianz to open a cloister with the intent of starting a home for the Salvatorian Fathers.

In 1907, a new monastery was blessed by a bishop from Green Bay, and in 1909, the college was opened. While the college only had nine students when it began, it continued to be a college and seminary for the Salvatorian order until 1969 when it shut down.

It was during the 1970s that the building reopened as JFK Prep Academy. This academy was short-lived as it discontinued operations in 1982. During this time period, numerous students reported encounters with ghostly apparitions.

In September of 2004, the property was purchased by Jerry Slavik of Commandments Mission LLC, who intends to revive the buildings by reopening the church, creating dormitory-style rental units, and creating an RV campsite.

Tabernacle Cemetery

Location: Waukesha, Waukesha County, Delafield Township, Wisconsin

Directions: From Waukesha, take Hwy 18 (Summit Ave) west, turn right on Cty Rd G (Elmhurst Dr), turn left on Bryn Dr, the Tabernacle Cemetery will be on the left.

Ghost Lore

There is a farm down the road from the cemetery, and a farmer's son accidentally hanged himself in the hayloft back in the 1840s. The boy was the first person buried on a nearby hill that later became the Tabernacle Cemetery. The farmer later painted the boy's name on the side of the barn.

- The apparition of a man has been seen standing next to the tree directly behind the cemetery sign.

- Bright flashes of light have been seen near the fence.

- After dark, mysterious headlights in the northwestern corner of the cemetery will often shine upon people.

The Dare: If you drive to the cemetery late at night, a mysterious truck will appear and follow you until you get back to the city.

Investigation

There is a privately owned farm across the road from the cemetery, but the barn there does not even date back to the 1840s, and contrary to the rumors, nobody ever died in this barn.

Warning:: *People who trespass on this property and/or van-*

The tree where the apparition has allegedly been spotted.

dalize the barn will be arrested!

We have learned that there was, indeed, a barn where a boy accidentally hanged himself, but it was not the barn adjacent to the cemetery. To protect the privacy of the land owners, we will not disclose the location of the barn where this actually did take place.

History

The cemetery was founded in 1842. It is not known who was the first person buried there. In 1845, a Welsh Congregational church built a log church on the hillside where the cemetery lies. In 1866, it was replaced by a small frame church about one-half mile to the southeast.

The fence where mysterious lights have reportedly been observed.

BIBLIOGRAPHY

Boyer, Dennis. *Driftless Spirits: Ghosts of Southwest Wisconsin.* Madison, WI: Prairie Oak Press, 1996.

Boyer, Dennis. *Gone Missing: A Supernatural Guide to the Great Lakes.* Oregon, WI: Badger Books, 2002.

Boyer, Dennis. *Northern Frights: A Supernatural Ecology of the Wisconsin Headwaters.* Madison, WI: Prairie Oak Press, 1998.

Feldman, Michael and Diana Cook. *Wisconsin Curiosities.* Guilford, CT: The Globe Pequot Press, 2000.

Gard, Robert E. and L.G. Sorden. *Wisconsin Lore.* Ashland, WI: Heartland Press, 1962.

Godfrey, Linda S. *The Beast of Bray Road: Tailing Wisconsin's Werewolf.* Black Earth, WI: Prairie Oak Press, 2003.

Godfrey, Linda. *The Poison Widow: A True Story of Sin, Strychnine, and Murder.* Black Earth, WI: Prairie Oak Press, 2003.

Hollatz, Tom. *The Haunted Northwoods.* St. Cloud, MN: North Star Press, 2000.

Leary, James P. (editor). *Wisconsin Folklore.* Madison, WI: The University of Wisconsin Press, 1998.

Levy, Hannah Heidi. *Famous Wisconsin Mystics.* Oregon, WI: Badger Books Inc., 2003.

Norman, Michael and Beth Scott. *Haunted America.* New York: A Tom Doherty Associates Book, 1994.

Norman, Michael and Beth Scott. *Haunted Heartland.* New York: Warner Books, 1985.

Norman, Michael & Beth Scott. *Haunted Heritage.* New York, NY: Tor Books, 2002.

Norman, Michael & Beth Scott. *Haunted Wisconsin.* Revised Edition. Black Earth, WI: Trails Books, 2001.

Rath, Jay. *The W-Files: True Reports of Wisconsin's Unexplained Phenomena.* Madison, WI: Wisconsin Trails, 1997.

Rider, Geri. *Ghosts of Door County.* Wisconsin, Quixote Press, 1992.

Pohlen, Jerome. *Oddball Wisconsin: A Guide to Some Really Strange Places.* Chicago, IL: Chicago Review Press, 2001.

von Bober, Wolffgang. *The Carver Effect: A Paranormal Experience.* Harris, PA: Stackpole Books, 1979.

INDEX

H

X

Y

Z

About the Authors

Chad Lewis is a paranormal investigator with a Master's degree in Applied Psychology from the University of Wisconsin–Stout. He works as a research specialist for the Mutual UFO Network, is a former member of the American Ghost Society, and works with BLT Crop Circle Investigations. Chad has organized and presented at numerous professional conferences, been featured in several video documentaries, and hosted *The Unexplained* paranormal radio talk show and television series. He is the author of *Eerie Eau Claire* and *Unexplained: From Angels to UFOs*. Chad's search for the paranormal has taken him to the far corners of the world. He has traveled to Area 51 in Nevada, Loch Ness in Scotland, Transylvania in Romania, Lough Ree in Ireland, and haunted castles and tunnels in London.

Terry Fisk is a paranormal investigator and area representative for the American Ghost Society. He is a shamanic Buddhist practitioner and member of the Foundation for Shamanic Studies, who studied Philosophy and Religion at the University of Wisconsin. Terry co-hosted *The Unexplained* paranormal radio talk show and is the director for *The Unexplained* television series.

ORDER BOOKS

To order additional copies of this book, send $14.00 (postage & handling included) to the following address:

Unexplained Research
PO Box 2173
Eau Claire, WI 54702-2173

Or visit our website:

www.unexplainedresearch.com